More early praise for Ri~~chard D.~~ Lewis
and *Finland, Cultural Lone Wolf*

"Having worked in Finland for the last twenty years, Richard Lewis's book is the best I have ever read on Finns and their culture. *Finland, Cultural Lone Wolf* is a fine appreciation of a fine people. For those wishing to better understand our northernmost EU neighbor, it is compulsory and compelling reading."

> —JOHN STUTTARD, CHAIRMAN, FINNISH-BRITISH
> CHAMBER OF COMMERCE, SENIOR CLIENT
> PARTNER, PRICEWATERHOUSECOOPERS
> AND ALDERMAN, CITY OF LONDON

"It is absolutely amazing how well Richard Lewis can penetrate the Finnish soul."

> —PERTTI SALOLAINEN, AMBASSADOR
> OF FINLAND IN THE UNITED KINGDOM

"With warmth and humor, Richard D. Lewis shows how Finland has emerged as one of the top leaders in the high-tech world of international business and become a respected player in the EU. Highly informative for anyone wanting to gain a better understanding of Finns and how they think, communicate and do business."

> —ULLA LADAU-HARJULIN, LECTURER IN
> INTERCULTURAL COMMUNICATION, FRSA,
> SWEDISH SCHOOL OF ECONOMICS AND BUSINESS
> ADMINISTRATION, HELSINKI, FINLAND

OTHER WORKS BY RICHARD D. LEWIS

BOOKS

When Cultures Collide, third edition (2006) Boston: Nicholas Brealey Publishing

English You Need (1958) Lisbon: Publitur

Suomen Kirja (1958) Helsinki: Berlitz

Vous-souvenez-vous (1959) Lisbon: Publitur

Reading for Adults (1968) London: Longman

Travelling Abroad (1971) Lisbon: Libraria Francisco Franco

Cambridge 2000 (1971) Lisbon: Linguasonica

The Billingers (1976) London: Riversdown Publications

Memoirs of a Linguist: The Road from Wigan Pier (1998) Winchester: Transcreen Publications

Cross-Cultural Communication: A Visual Approach (1999) Winchester: Transcreen Publications

The Cultural Imperative: Global Trends in the 21st Century (2002) Yarmouth, ME: Intercultural Press

Humour across Frontiers (2005) Winchester: Transcreen Publications

MULTIMEDIA

Englantia Hauskaa ja Helppoa (film series) (1961) Finnish Television

Walter and Connie (film series) (1962) London: BBC

Transcreen English (video series) (1988) Winchester: Transcreen Educational Films

Gulliver: Performing Successfully Across Cultures (1999) (CD-ROM and intranet training tool) London: Richard Lewis Communications

National Cultural Profiles and Cultural Assessment (2002) (Web-based support system) London: CultureActive

Richard D. Lewis is available as a cross-cultural trainer, consultant, speaker, and language specialist in the subjects covered in this book. He can be reached at:

Richard Lewis Communications
Riversdown House
Wamford, Hampshire SO32 3LH
United Kingdom
e-mail: info@crossculture.com
phone: +44-1962-77-1111
fax: +44-1962-77-1050
Website: www.crossculture.com

FINLAND, Cultural Lone Wolf

Richard D. Lewis

INTERCULTURAL PRESS
A Nicholas Brealey Publishing Company

BOSTON • LONDON

First published by Intercultural Press, a Nicholas Brealey Publishing Company in 2005

Intercultural Press, Inc.
A Nicholas Brealey Publishing Company
53 State Street, 9th Floor
Boston, MA 02109, USA
Tel: 617-523-3801
Fax: 617-523-3708

Nicholas Brealey Publishing
Carmelite House
50 Victoria Embankment
London EC4Y 0DZ
Tel: 020 3122 6000

www.nicholasbrealey.com

Printed in the United States of America

22 21 20 19   10 11 12 13

ISBN: 978-1-931930-18-5

Library of Congress Cataloging-in-Publication Data

Lewis, Richard D.
    Finland, cultural lone wolf / Richard D. Lewis.—1st ed.
      p. cm.
    Includes bibliographical references and index.
      ISBN 1-931930-18-X (alk. paper)
    1. Finland.   I. Title.
      DL1012.L48 2005
      948.97—dc22

                                            2004021973

To Norman Taylor and Nelly Soininen

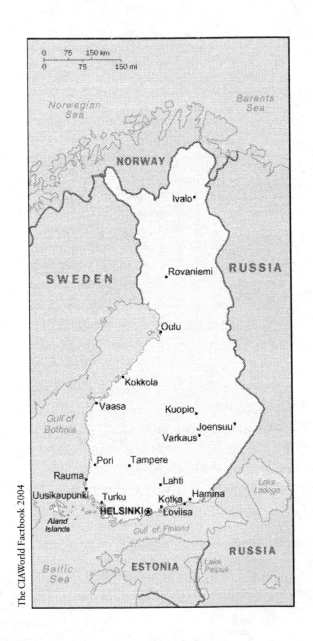

CONTENTS

ACKNOWLEDGMENTS

No account of Finland or the Finns escapes the influence of Max Jacobson and Matti Klinge, whose penetrating historical insights have been my chief sources of information and inspiration. Both highlight the singular, often solitary, course steered by a succession of Finnish governments as the Finns pursue their destiny, not as compliant pawns of the Great Powers but on their own autonomous terms.

If the title of this book reflects this distinctive characteristic, it is because I believe it is an ineluctable product of Finnish culture, unique in its unswerving, implacable values; its synthetic language and thought patterns; its own notions of form, shape, color, music, and poetry; and its assumptions of right and wrong. The Finnish philosopher J. V. Snellman wrote that a nation's power is in its culture.

My evaluation of "Finnishness" has been influenced by the writings of Snellman, Runeberg, Väinö Linna, Mika Waltari and the memoirs of Marshal C. G. E. Mannerheim. I have also learned from essays by Seppo Tiitinen ("Internationalising Parliament"), Allan Tiitta ("A Land of Many Faces"), and Seppo Zetterberg ("Finland through the Centuries") for historical and geographical details, and from Kaija Valkonen's description of aspects of Finnish culture ranging from Lönnrot's *Kalevala* to modern architecture and design. Martti Korhonen helped me compile some statistics regarding the Finnish education system and the Parliament. Patrick

Humphreys' *Finland in a Small Book* raised some interesting questions often asked about Finns. The chapter on Finnish leadership was written in conjunction with Michael Gates. In Chapter 15, "The Wily Weasel," I have leaned heavily on the excellent and comprehensive account of Nokia by Martti Häikiö ("Nokia, The Inside Story").

In the chapter on Finnish origins, I have relied on research and analyses carried out by scholars and scientists such as H. R. Nevanlinna, L. L. Cavalli-Sforza, P. Dolukhanov, K. Wiik, and C. R. Guglielmino as well as recent comprehensive articles on Finland's prehistory by Markku Niskanen, Kyösti Julku, and Milton Nuñez. Besides acknowledging the guidance I have received from the above works, I would also like to thank Judy Carl-Hendrick, managing editor, for her thoughtful support, as well as Patricia O'Hare, publisher, and the rest of the staff at Intercultural Press.

Finally, as author, I take full responsibility for any and all errors that may have inadvertently found their way into the book.

PREFACE

This book is being published at a time when Finland leads the world in various fields of technology, network readiness, global competitiveness, research and creativity, reading, mathematical and scientific literacy, enrollments in universities and colleges, empowerment of women, and sustainability of the environment.

At cross-century, articles in British and American publications appeared with titles like "The Future Is Finnish." Finland has also become a key European Union (EU) player between the EU, Russia, and the Baltic States.

How Finland, by pursuing a "Lone Wolf" policy, achieved such progress from a war-battered standing and struggling economy in 1945 is the story of this book. My fifty years spent in Finland have enabled me to write about this land with some confidence, but my insights into the Finnish character would have been inadequate had I not met, learned to know, and befriended a wide variety of twentieth-century Finns who have generously shared their experiences and worldview with me. These include some of my former students such as Prime Minister Johannes Virolainen, as well as other parliamentarians like Markus Aaltonen, Kari Ahonen, Eero Heinäluoma, Ilkka Kanerva, Martti Korhonen, Mikko Pesälä, and Seppo Tiitinen; and ministry officials Aila Gorski, Asko Lindqvist, Marja Paavilainen, Ilkka Ruska, and Erkki Virtanen. In the worlds of sport, drama, and art I became acquainted with Kalevi Häkkinen, Åke Lindman, Carita Mattila, Timo Sarpaneva, Lasse Virén,

Kauko Vuorensola, and Wille Zilliacus. My involvement with Finnish business and industry allowed me to meet Eero Ahola, Pekka Ala-Pietilä, Hakon Borup, Klaus Cawén, Tauno Matomäki, Jouko Leskinen, Jukka Härmälä, Antti Herlin, Jussi Huttunen, Jaakko Ihamuotila, Jarl Köhler, Juhani Kuusi, Eero Leivo, Matti Lounasmeri, Kari Mattila, Aulis Salin, Keijo Suila, Matti Sundberg, Pirkko Tuomisto, Markku Vartiainen, Kari Vainio, Maunu von Lueders, Eero Vuohula, Tapio Wartiovaara, and many other personable Finnish-speaking and Swedish-speaking Finns. To all of them I am grateful for the moments they shared with me. None has intensified my affection for Finland more than Pertti Salolainen, Finnish ambassador to the United Kingdom from 1996 to the present day. Salolainen, from whom I received my decoration, is a committed Anglophile, exuding warmth and humanity; he typifies more than anyone I know the staunch, loyal soul of the bleak northern territory I describe in the following pages.

Finland's international standing and security are increased in direct proportion to the deepening knowledge and awareness of the country by foreign peoples. If, by recounting in this book the characteristics, strengths, progress, and advances of the Finnish people, I have been able to highlight to some degree their merits and achievements, that will be my chief source of satisfaction in writing these words.

RDL

INTRODUCTION:
A Country Apart

Once upon a time, long long ago, there was a far-off land close to the Arctic Circle—a chilly, bleak patchwork of forests and lakes, where bears, wolves, elks, and lynxes roamed freely and where Christmases were always white.

A strange tribe from faraway arrived in this land, where no other people had chosen to live, and set about the task of making themselves comfortable there. They cut wood to construct dwellings, they planted crops on open land, and they fished the lakes and rivers.

They were an unusual people: of an independent nature, devoted to hard work, yet modest in their aspirations and jealous of their honest reputation. They were clean in their habits, physically fit, and enjoyed the outdoor life. They spoke very little, for loquaciousness and especially boasting were taboo. Solitude was the safest, and they loved the great space that the new land offered.

Like other peoples, they had jealous neighbors, and they had to fight many battles to defend their territory. They did not always win and were subjugated for long periods. Notwithstanding their suffering and humiliation, they never gave up; in the end they made their land secure and have lived happily there up to the present day.

If this sounds like a fairy tale, it is perhaps because it possesses the elements of one, but we are talking about a modern nation that really exists. This nation, clinging to the old values in the fairy tale, fought a modern giant (state) of two hundred million people to hold on to what we today call a democracy. The honest tribe continues to pay off all its debts, protect its environment, and vanquish crime, injustice, and poverty. The quiet people solve modern problems such as treatment of its minorities, resettlement of refugees (400,000 Karelians), and pollution without any fuss.

The tribe is still not very well known in the lands to the south and its people are notoriously poor at blowing their own trumpet. Their Altaic language does not calibrate with the majority of the world's tongues. Their basic shyness and dislike of exhibitionism lend thickness to an intervening curtain of cultural complexity, voluntary withdrawal, and geographical remoteness. They feel a sense of separateness from other peoples.

Yet this tribe is warmhearted, wishing to be loved, and anxious to join the rest of us. They are energetic, essentially inventive, and have much to offer others. We should do well to study this enigmatic, sometimes maverick, always caring, reliable people.

These few words are intended as a message of congratulation to the Finnish people (yes, it is Finland we are talking about!) for what they have achieved so far and for what they are destined to achieve in the future. Somebody must blow their trumpet for them, just a little.

THE GOLD MEDAL COUNTRY

If you ask someone which country ranks first in global competitiveness in business, the most common answer would be the U.S. or Singapore or Japan. All would be wrong. It's Finland. Finland? Surely someone has made a statistical mistake, or is it a flash in the pan?

Not so. The Growth Competitiveness Index ranking by the World Economic Forum placed Finland first already in 2001, followed by the U.S., Canada, Singapore, and Australia. But that was only for starters. In 2003 Finland outranked the U.S., Singapore, and all others in global competitiveness, reflecting the ability of a country to sustain its high rates of growth based on 259 criteria, including the openness of the economy, technology, government policies, and integration into trade blocks.

Will they be able to maintain their lead?

It would seem so. Such respected journals as *The Economist* and the *Financial Times* have recently entitled articles "The Future Is Finnish."

What are the grounds for such an assumption?

They are numerous. Finns seem to invest their efforts (and often their money) in areas designed to guarantee a healthy and prosperous future. Starting with education, they came first in an Organisation for Economic Cooperation and Development (OECD) survey of European standards of reading and mathematical and scientific literacy (2003). Worldwide, only the Koreans matched them in these fundamental skills. In Europe, Finland leads all other countries in postsecondary enrollments by 12 percent.

Do they plan on remaining the best-educated people on the continent?

In the world, in fact. They are in the top two countries in the economic creativity index, and they are trailing only Sweden and are well ahead of the U.S. in research and development (R&D) spending (as a percentage of GDP). They are global leaders in e-banking, have the highest Internet and mobile phone penetration, have a 100 percent digital fiber-optic network, and are home to 10 percent of all Europe's new medical biotechnology companies.

All this sounds pretty high tech, but more than that, they are high tech where it counts. Apart from their dominance in mobile phone technology, information technology (IT), and pulp and paper products, they have secured their environmental future by concentrating on such issues as water management, human vulnerability to environmental risks, resource sharing, and assimilation of waste.

All this leads one to the conclusion that their future is very bright indeed. They are easily number one in the Economist Environmental Sustainability Index (2004). Only Norway, Sweden, and Canada come close. As is generally recognized, the supply of clean water is one of the vital issues of this century. Finland heads the list in access, supply, use, resources, and environmental impact.

What about the economy?

Strategically situated between Russia and the EU, also with good markets in the U.S., Finland is pretty well balanced. It was not just by chance that in 2000 Nokia was Europe's biggest company by capitalization. But surely Nokia is Japanese? Not so. Nokia is Finnish born and bred, operating on Finnish turf and until recently with an all-Finnish board of directors.

If one asks how a Finnish company could grow bigger than Volkswagen, Mercedes-Benz, and Fiat, not to mention Unilever and Shell, the answer is in research. In 2001, Nokia employed 18,600 people in R&D at 54 centers in 14 different countries.

Can one suppose that the combination of educational superiority and technological research will enable Finland to continue as a world leader in so many fields?

This is extremely likely, especially as they lead other nations in moral strengths.

What does that mean?

According to up-to-date surveys, Finland tops the league in the Corruption Free Index, are the fastest payers in the European Union, and lead the world in minimal bureaucracy. They are an understated society in an era of hype, media hysteria, and abuse; they prize modesty and straight talking above most other attributes. Paavo Lipponen, the prime minister at cross-century, was voted the least charismatic Finnish politician; he shunned hype and small talk, preferring to do his job seriously. What country other than Finland would have fired the following prime minister, Anneli Jäätteenmäki, because she was guilty of a questionable untruth in her remarks to Parliament? (Think what Berlusconi and Chirac get away with.)

What other country would have fined a young Finnish Internet whiz-kid $75,000 for speeding (linking the fine to his sizeable income)? Another Finnish whiz-kid, Linus Torvalds, the inventor of the Linux operating system, which rivals mammoth Microsoft, was hardly interested in profits, preferring Linux excellence to reflect Finland's model of social welfare. One senior Microsoft executive attacked Torvalds for being "un-American"!

Finnish humility and honesty were praised unequivocally in the *Harvard Business Review* by Manfred Kets deVries, Director of

INSEAD's Global Leadership Centre, who admired the Finnish style of management more than any other.

Finns are characterized by fresh and innovative thinking that enhances their national image. They tackle serious subjects, such as care of the young (they are third lowest in the world in infant mortality). In the last few years the Finnish government provided strong leadership to eliminate obesity among school children. By planning the food for free school lunches, child obesity was rapidly cut to 11 percent (cf. Britain, 22 percent).

Finns seem to be a nation of "doers" rather than talkers. What are the secrets of their success?

Finns are mainly silent people who go in for deep thinking, which is facilitated by the synthetic nature of their language. Silence engenders vision, imagination, and calm judgments. Small talk interferes with creative thought. Finns take talking seriously and prefer to use language for something that actually pushes things further on the pragmatic level. The basic rule is "less is more." Finns are adept at creating formulas that enable them to cope with complex political, social, and economic situations. Their originality is bolstered by consistent pragmatism—see how they prefer to be straight to the point, shunning any form of hype—letting the technical story do the talking.

Why is their English so good?

Another pragmatic decision. It's the world language. The French, Italians, and Spaniards will pay for their neglect of English in twenty-first-century business. Finns have an obsession with achieving and have created something new to cement achievement: one writer described it as "Finnish world-classness." The Finnish government helps in promoting this by making decisions of national importance through a "rainbow coalition" (effective since the early 1990s) where all parties respect harmonious relations between industry, academia, and government.

How did a country with no natural resources except trees and long-distance runners succeed in distinguishing itself so strikingly?

Two basic strengths are responsible: Properly managed forest is an ever-replenishing source of riches. And as for the runners, which country won most Olympic medals per capita? It must be the United States. Not exactly. The U.S. is in sixteenth place with 8.3 medals per million inhabitants. Norway is third with 53.1 medals. Sweden is second with 56.3. Any guesses for first? Finland perhaps? Right—106 medals per million.

FINNISH ORIGINS

*"A strange tribe from faraway arrived in this land, where
no other people had chosen to live."*

This simple statement of fact—true though it is—is also of an enigmatic nature. How strange was this tribe? From how far away had
they come? Who exactly were the Finns? Who were their relatives?
How and when did they reach this empty territory and why was
it empty, or was it really empty? Which lands did the Finns pass
through en route, and why did they not stop off in friendlier climes?
If, as it seems, they are linguistically related to the Estonians, Lapps,
and Hungarians, how and why did the Hungarians end up on the
Danube? What is the significance of these four tribes speaking
Finno-Ugrian languages when the rest of Europe's forty countries
express themselves in dominant Indo-European tongues? How
on earth have the Finnic languages managed to maintain for thousands of years a linguistic toehold in a bleak and remote corner of
northeastern Europe, all the while subjected to enormous cultural
and political pressures from the Scandinavian west and the Slavic
east? When European languages such as Etruscan, Pictish, Cornish,
Pelasgian, and ancient Iberian and Sicilian have disappeared, why
are the Finno-Ugrian tongues so resilient that Finnish was, in 1995,
accepted as one of the fifteen official languages of the European
Union?

Theories of Origin

If indeed the questions asked above appear numerous, far-reaching, and probing, it is because the provenance and origins of the Finnish people are shrouded in the mists of historical and prehistoric time, in no less mystery than that which accompanies the roots and routes of the much larger and more widespread family of peoples, their neighbors the Indo-Europeans.

When the Bona Ventura paper, published in 1597, revealed the affinities of the German and Persian languages, a door was opened to over 400 years of speculation as to the original homeland of the Indo-Europeans. So far none of the three hundred or more hypotheses put forward has gained a widely accepted endorsement.

A parallel discussion regarding the homeland of the Finno-Ugrian peoples has been held for less time than the Indo-European debate (about 150 years), partly on account of the relatively late emergence of the Finnish state, but more particularly because of the establishment and predominance of one hypothesis that can be called the "Migration Theory."

The Migration Theory

According to the migration hypothesis, the Finns migrated from a homeland in northwestern Siberia close to the Ural Mountains. They spoke a Uralic tongue (Finno-Ugrian is related to Uralian and possibly Altaic languages), and they had a Mongoloid element because the ancestral Uralic people were Mongoloids. The migration, which left Finno-Ugrian linguistic footprints all the way from the Urals to the shores of the Baltic, entered its semifinal stages in Estonia and southern Finland around 1000 B.C., about when the Finns separated from the Estonians.

This highly romanticist hypothesis, heroic in terms of territory traversed and its chainlike family of Finno-Ugrian-speaking relatives, held sway in academia for the best part of a century. Its origin was the discovery, by Friedrich Blumenbach, a prominent eighteenth-

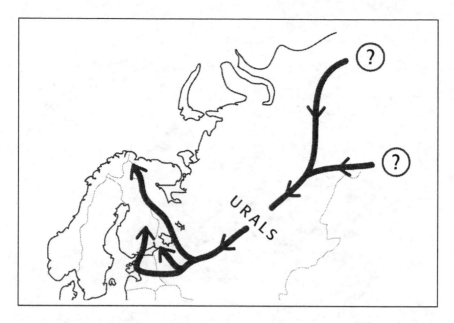

FIGURE 2.1   The Migration Theory

century scientist and anthropologist, of one Finnish and two Lappish skulls that bore marked resemblances to one Mongol skull in
Blumenbach's possession. This Mongoloid affinity of the Finno-
Ugrians was accepted as scientific truth, largely because it received
considerable support from linguists.

The Migration Theory (see Figure 2.1), linguist-friendly and
neat in many of its assumptions, has come under heavy attack since
the 1980s from a number of science-based sources. Enter the geneti-
cists, archeologists, and craniologists.

The Settlement Continuity Theory

Although there is adequate evidence to confirm the arrival of the
Baltic Finns (including the Estonians) in the Baltic area about three
thousand years ago, scientific advances in research suggest that this
was by no means the beginning of settlement in Finland. Not only
were these groups latecomers to Finland's shores but also they may
not have been the first Finno-Ugrians to arrive, either.

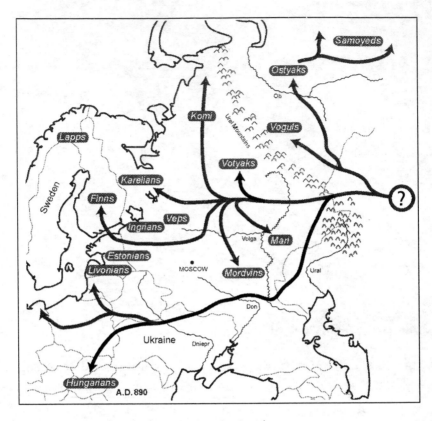

FIGURE 2.2   The Settlement Continuity Theory

To set the scene for the Settlement Continuity Theory, we have to roll back not only centuries, but millennia. We are aware of three great ice ages in Europe, but we need focus only on the last Glacial Maximum, when all of northern Eurasia was covered by a mighty ice sheet from 23,000 to 19,500 B.C. Northern Europe in its entirety, certainly including Finland, was uninhabited at this time. When the Nordic ice finally retreated after 19,500 B.C., the mammals and birds followed it northward, as conditions permitted. The humans advanced north again, slowly and unevenly. Who were these humans of twenty thousand years ago? What was their culture and language(s)? Were they Proto-Uralians, Proto-Indo-Europeans, or other ancient groups?

Our answers to most of these questions are inevitably incomplete, although we learn more as time goes by. We know, however, that the ice, retreating at a speed of about twenty-five kilometers a generation, started to render southern Finland ice-free around 9000 B.C. The southern half of Finland was populated by 8000 B.C. and northernmost Finland by 7500 B.C. Again, the question is posed: Who were they? What was their language/culture?

An Interesting Rendezvous

When the improving climatic conditions enabled our hardy vanguard of north-pushing Finns to begin to colonize the northern extremity of Finland around 7500–8000 B.C., they may have been surprised to meet another group who had arrived in northern Fennoscandia as early as 9000 B.C. from what was then an ice-free region between the British Isles, Denmark, and southern Norway. Although inland Scandinavia was still under an ice sheet, the Norwegian coast was ice-free, enabling the coastal groups to reach the Arctic. The coastal groups formed a mingling community of Saami (Lapps) and northern-bound settlers who between them established a Proto-Uralic tongue as the language of the area. Recent biological evidence shows the Lapps to be genetically very distinct from Scandinavians and Baltic Finns, but such a mingling around 7500 B.C. would explain how Lapps and Finns, though genetically distant, speak closely related languages. One of the groups most likely assimilated the other (although we cannot rule out the possibility that all the relevant linguistic elements were Proto-Uralian).

At all events, Proto-Uralian or Finno-Ugrian ancestral tongues led to Finnish being established, along with its dialects, in the expanse of land between the Gulf of Bothnia and Lake Ladoga. Why, then, should we quarrel with the basic logic of the Migration Theory, which linguists were satisfied with for over a hundred years? If Finns speak a language that is unquestionably Asian, why should we doubt their Asian provenance? Because genetic markers tell us otherwise.

The Genetic Evidence

Modern research of human biological variation examines how natural selection, climatic selection, and migrations affect the genetic structures of populations over generations. Genetic structures can be used to reconstruct a people's history and genetic relationships. In line with the Migration Theory, it was assumed that the Finns would have close genetic affinities with the eastern Finno-Ugrian-speaking populations. However, Professor Markku Niskanen of Oulu University demonstrated conclusively in papers presented in the period 1994–1998 that studies of genetic relationships among Northern and Central Europeans indicated that Baltic Finns had much closer genetic affinities with their Scandinavian neighbors than with the eastern Finno-Ugrians. The closeness to Scandinavians suggests that the ancestors of the Baltic Finns have more likely lived in the Baltic region for 10,000 years, rather than 3,000, and probably arrived from the south rather than from the east. Moreover, similar studies carried out on the Lapps showed that they too are genetically typical Europeans. The genetic distances between the Finns and the Lapps are smaller than those between the Lapps and other Europeans, though still quite large. Findings demonstrate clearly European gene pools for Finns, Estonians, and even the easternmost Finno-Ugrians.

In short, the genetic closeness of the Finns to the Swedes and Danes (and even to the British) lends strong anthropological support to the Settlement Continuity Theory, according to which the Finno-Ugrians were very likely the hunter/gatherers who inhabited the periglacial zone during the last Glacial Maximum. Their movement north following the retreating ice would be from the south and much more from the west than the Migration Theory had indicated.

The Indo-Europeans

One thing we know for certain about the Finns and other Finno-Ugrians is that they are not Indo-European in origin. The sweep of Indo-European languages is very great; not only are these tongues spoken in forty countries in Europe, but they are very much alive in Iran, Tajikistan, and large parts of northern India. Hindi, Urdu, Bengali, Punjabi, and Persian are closely related Indo-European tongues.

The invention of farming between the Tigris and Euphrates Rivers in present-day Iraq, its spread westward, and the associated domestication and breeding of animals (particularly the horse) gave a tremendous boost to the Indo-Europeans, whose homeland we cannot definitely pinpoint. The spread of the Indo-European peoples and languages to the west was in all probability along latitudes south of the Finno-Ugrians. Their march was unstoppable to the extent that all other groups in Central and Southern Europe were pushed aside or assimilated. Linguistically, they took everything before them. In the end the only two non-Indo-European languages to survive were Basque and the Caucasian language(s) spoken in the mountain strongholds of the Pyrenees and the Caucasians. Apart from Finno-Ugrian, of course.

Over the last thirty years, scientific research in various disciplines, such as physical anthropology, craniometric analyses, nuclear genetic markers, mitochondrial DNA, Y-chromosomal DNA, and allele frequencies, has thrown its weight behind the Finno-Ugrian Settlement Continuity Theory and consequently reduced the likelihood of a major westward migration as recent as 3,000 years ago. The Finns and Finno-Ugrians in general have lighter coloring (skin, eyes, hair) than any other human beings, which shows they have lived in Northern Europe the longest. The hypothesis arises that the Finno-Ugrians can stake a valid claim to be among the early indigenous inhabitants of Europe.

This hypothesis carries with it considerable importance in our evaluation of the Finns' position in the modern European setting. The Migration Theory in a sense relegated the Finns to the minor role of Asian immigrants clinging tenaciously to a little-desired corner of a continent occupied by dynamic Indo-European settlers. The Settlement Continuity Theory turns this notion on its head. What we have instead is a scenario of Proto-Uralian or Finno-Ugrian precedence in a wide-ranging European cultural mainstream, entered into at a later date by Indo-Europeans emanating from the east. Of course, things are infinitesimally more complex than that, and much of the above debate, including some of the deductions derived from scientific research, are largely speculative. This is always the case when we weigh the events of prehistory.*

However, it is tempting to link the spectacular progress and success of the Finnish people in the short time since their independence, and particularly at cross-century, with the fine European pedigree that the above considerations hint at.

Do they deserve anything less?

---

*Readers wishing to see a more fully documented version of Finnish origins should go to http://www.crossculture.com/lonewolf/origins

GEOGRAPHICAL OVERVIEW

Among the factors contributing to the creation and directionality of a culture, history and geography are high on the list. Of the two, geography—more implacable and primary—often dominates. Finnish history, like that of other nations, has unrolled and evolved within a geographical framework and context (in this case an austere one). In a sense, geography was first; in that severe environment the Finns carved out their history.

One cannot overestimate the importance of geographic conditions, including climate, and their influence on the development of the Finnish mindset. A question often asked is why the Finnish people chose this broad expanse of land lying between the Gulf of Bothnia, the Gulf of Finland, and Lake Ladoga to eke out their precarious existence. What tempted them to claim their country on land lying in its entirety about 60°N? Nobody else did, except for the Icelanders, who were originally outlaws. When one experiences the ample chunk of northern Finland where winter darkness (*kaamos*) reigns for fifty-two consecutive days and where temperatures plummet to −40°C, one also asks why they stayed.

There are other inhospitable parts of the earth, in the Arctic or in desert environments, where inhabitants have demonstrated tenacity in clinging to land that could barely support survival; fixedness and a sedentary nature are stubborn traits found among some peoples. Where the Finns differ in such comparisons is in their indisputable success in creating a modern state, sophisticated in all aspects—social and artistic, economic, industrial, administrative, political, and technological. We cannot know for sure why the Finns chose to settle this territory. One reason may be simply because it was empty. Also they already had a northern provenance. They may have persisted in such austere conditions on the principle of "What we have we hold."

To what extent did the geographical environment mold the Finnish character and contribute, in a positive or negative manner, to the people's development and growth? To gain the full perspective, one has to step back in time—about 10,000 years. We have seen in the previous chapter how the Finnish ancestral hunter-gatherers followed the receding ice from 8000 B.C. onward into what is now Finnish territory. What did it look like? What encouraged them to pursue a northern route? Probably it was lack of resistance.

Even today, for many months of the year, large parts of Finland have a forbidding aspect to some. If one were to choose a few adjectives to describe the topography, words such as *bleak, cold, barren, gray, dark,* and *waterlogged* might come to mind. The ice ages were not kind to Finland. The granite bedrock so visible in the forests had once been the base of a range of sizeable mountains in the Precambrian period. The very antiquity of the rock and its subsequent erosion over eons of time produced the flat topography characterizing Finland today. In the most recent periods of glaciation, the topsoil was scraped off by the huge glaciers and pushed southward to Central and South Europe. Finnish territory was left with an abundance of surface bedrock, with a thin covering of soil providing meager possibilities for cultivation. Water filled the millions of crevasses carved out by the glaciers—hence the waterlogged aspect of the topography. More than 10 percent of Finland is permanently under water. Mires and quagmires are proportionately higher than anywhere else in the world.

Finland has 188,000 lakes, the Saimaa Lake area being Europe's biggest inland water system. The drenched landscape produced a total of 179,584 Finnish islands, about 100,000 of which protrude from the lakes. Another 80,000 dot Finnish coasts, forming the largest archipelago in the Northern Hemisphere, between Sweden and Finland. Åland is bigger than thirteen independent states. If one takes into consideration poor-growth forest adjacent to swamps, wetlands constitute almost one-third of Finnish territory. These freeze in winter, as does the sea several miles out from the coast. All in all, a bleak outlook for our newly arrived hunter-gatherer in 8000 B.C.

In fact, things were not that bad. Immediately after the last ice age, Northern Europe was much warmer than it is today. Oak and beech forests stretched to the north of Finland, where today only stunted conifers and birch can grow. In the absence of agriculture, hunting and fishing were the primary activities. The mammals preceded the people, following the receding ice. Elks, reindeer, bears, foxes, weasels, hares, and wolves are among 60–70 mammal species, while there are more than 350 species of birds. Fish were plentiful, both in the lakes and in the Baltic. Lapland rivers were home to various types of salmon. Throughout history, humans have followed game; for more than 90 percent of their existence, hunting and fishing have been the chief means of survival.

As our pioneering Finns pushed northward to the Arctic Ocean for a thousand years, their battle with the environment was contemporaneous with those of other groups in different parts of the world. In the Americas, Indians had crossed the Bering Strait in 12,000 B.C. and had reached Tierra del Fuego at least three millennia before Finland was settled. They too had battled the elements in a far richer but immeasurably more complicated geographical environment than the Finnish. In Australia, the Aborigines were already

35,000 years into their Dreamtime, facing the privations of a climate no less harsh than that of the Finns, but of a very different nature.

In Southeast Asia and Polynesia, inhabited even before 30,000 B.C., nature had a kinder face, producing a different, less challenged type of human. By 6000–5000 B.C. Chinese civilization was acquiring sophistication, and in the Fertile Crescent the invention and establishment of agriculture greatly facilitated human advancement. Released from the treadmill of chasing game to survive, the inhabitants of the Middle East and later Egypt and South and Central Europe developed extensive farming systems and a sedentary existence, enabling them to develop administrative and political skills as well as techniques to guarantee a steady supply of food. Finns, with their rock-and-water topography, were denied these luxuries. The transition from hunting to farming occurred very late in the Nordic area.

The pioneers of Finnish settlement in the postglacial period leading up to the time of Christ were, like other contemporary cultural groups, highly developed humans in the biological sense. Our Finnish settlers were intelligent, efficient, and cunning hunters, adapting to the inclement geographical conditions and increasing cold and showing no signs of retreat. Meat, fish, and berries were on offer for the resourceful individual or group. The intense cold, though hard to endure, minimized pestilence and plant diseases. It also reduced incursions into the territory by newcomers, and those who did make it into Finland were small enough in number to be assimilated (and learn Proto-Finnish!). The land, moreover, was expanding; the removal of the great weight of the ice sheet allowed Finnish territory to grow by approximately seven square kilometers per annum on its western coast. Winter nights were long, but so were the days of summer (Northern Finland has twenty-four-hour-a-day sunshine for over sixty days per year).

These environmental consolations notwithstanding, the fact remains that Finnish climate and topography present a formidable challenge to the inhabitants of the area. Centuries of conditioning and adaptation are reflected in Finnish behavior. Foreigners in Finland are struck by the taciturnity of the males. Low temperatures necessitate outdoor succinctness. One does not dally on the street at 20°C below freezing, and acquaintances meeting each other are likely to restrict their conversation to twenty seconds *en passant.* The same applies to their approach to strangers, though they may give you half a minute if you need the emergency ward of a hospital or wish to report a double murder to the police. Outdoor laughing and smiling are not part of the winter scene. A broad American smile at 15°C below in a Helsinki easterly makes one's front teeth ache.

This outdoor "winter behavior," as the Finns call it, carries over to their indoor communication habits, where economy of expression and the ability to summarize are prized. Norwegians living at the same latitudes exhibit this same tendency, aided by their terse Scandinavian (Norwegians, Swedes, and Danes are Nordic and Scandinavian; Finns are Nordic, not Scandinavian) language with its abundance of monosyllabic and bisyllabic words. Finnish is much more flowery, but Finnish males make up for this by remaining silent. Further references to Finnish taciturnity are made in Chapter 6.

Other by-products of this economy of expression are the lack of visible jocularity, dislike of gossip, preference for facts and figures, paucity of networking in comparison with Southern Europeans, and reduced eye contact. Sunny Greece and Spain have the strongest eye contact in Europe. Finns, used to cold winds whipping their face, often speak outdoors with narrowed eyes and frequently avoid prolonged eye contact during indoor conversations.

Much has been made of the Finns' penchant toward suicide and its possible link with bleak weather. Sunny Italians, Greeks, and Spaniards commit suicide least. Finns rank high in the suicide league, being surpassed only by their fellow Finno-Ugrians, the Hungarians. Finnish women, however, kill themselves less often than female Belgians, Swiss, Austrians, Danes, and Japanese. Factors other than climatological ones must contribute to suicidal tendencies. Alcoholism certainly plays a part, as do the long periods of darkness. Studies have found that Seasonal Affective Disorder (SAD) leads to depressed behavior. It seems paucity of light leads to the brain producing a different set of chemicals affecting moods. One notices the Finns' craving for sunshine and beach holidays (also common among other Nordics and British people).

Seventy percent of Finland is forested—an area larger than England. In fact, Finland is the most densely forested land in Europe. This too has an effect on the national character. It is often said that in many parts of Finland you can't see anything for the trees. This means that apart from those living in the cities and the few arable areas, Finns can be described as forest-dwellers (and were more so in times past). Forest-dwellers tend to be less outgoing than occupants of open land and value their privacy more.

Forest-dwelling usually leads to introspective behavior. Among trees, horizons are limited. Wide vistas may encourage imagination and charisma; when these are impeded by thick woods, people tend to develop *inner* horizons, engendering introversion, self-reliance, independence, and unhurried, deeper thinking. Finland is, as might be guessed, sparsely populated. The population ratio per square kilometer is the third lowest in Europe after Norway and Iceland. Finns' love of solitude and antipathy to physical closeness are well known. This is reflected by the existence (today) of 400,000 country houses (second homes), where Finns flee the bustle of the towns over the weekend.

Finnish rural log cabins are usually warm, cozy constructions with thick walls insulating the occupants not only from the cold but also from outsiders. With privacy at a premium, owners build their rural dwellings as far as possible from neighbors, often out of sight. Neighborliness eventually develops, but is not hurriedly sought. Self-efficiency is the name of the game; a do-it-yourself mentality is common among Finns.

Urbanized Finns, particularly in Helsinki, are more outgoing, and in recent years are characterized by a refreshing international outlook. However, Finnish males of all categories maintain a modicum of reserve in their relations with foreign people both in the way they communicate with them and in the freedom they allow foreigners within Finland's borders.

Foreign scholars and technical experts find a warm welcome, but the extremely low numbers of foreigners granted residence in Finland (0.4 percent of the population) reflects the age-old stance of the Arctic survivor keeping a wary eye on incursions from outside. As I mentioned earlier, the small numbers of foreign people infiltrating over the centuries were invariably assimilated and "Finnicized." A Romany community of nine thousand was moved into Finland during Swedish rule in the seventeenth century. They have made little impact on national life. The 5,000 Somalis admitted in the latter part of the twentieth century find the cold hard to bear. The 5,000-odd Lapps in Finland's northern region are accepted as fellow Arctic survivors.

The Finnish landscape reflects in some ways the east-west-north dimensions of Finnish culture. The southwest features deciduous trees, such as oaks and beech. The central and eastern regions are known for their thick conifer forests and ubiquitous lakes. The extreme north has barren fells with only stunted dwarf birch and firs. Modern Finns are the inheritors of an austere environment that caused their ancestors considerable hardship. The closed, often withdrawn nature of the people is a product of this hardy self-containment.

In summary, the influence of geography has been decisive and clearly positive. Cold latitudes engender cool, sturdy, resilient individuals with an inordinate capacity for self-reliance and a survival instinct. The Arctic survivor must have stamina, guts (*sisu*), self-dependence, and powers of invention.

It would seem that the farther from the equator one travels, the more industriousness one finds. Finns, the northernmost peoples, have consistently demonstrated their work ethic, tenacity, bravery in war, and cool pragmatism in peace. Their closeness to their barren land has given them a deep ecological awareness. Their forests are sustainable, their mammals largely unthreatened; they lead the world in water management. If you ask them if they are satisfied with or comfortable in their stern, rigorous, uncompromising existence, they will tell you, frankly, they would not live anywhere else.

HISTORICAL OVERVIEW

While Finland's credentials as a cultural lone wolf—a European nation with a unique Uralic language and communication style and Eastern and Arctic ingredients in her music, art and painting, literature, and artifacts—characterize her reputation, her stand-alone tendency has often led to her isolation in other spheres. This was never more evident than in 1939 when she was the victim of a surprise attack by the Soviet Union. Britain and the U.S. saw Finland as David fighting Goliath, but Anglo-Saxon sympathy notwithstanding, Finland did not receive substantial help from that quarter, neither from Germany nor her Nordic neighbors, in spite of a steady cementing of relations with these countries in the twenty-two years since independence. During the Winter War, which lasted four months, Finland was a lone wolf militarily, tenacious in self-defense, but having to concede 10 percent of her territory to achieve an uneasy truce.

Throughout her history, Finland's status and standing, her alignments, her enigmatic character, her very appeal have been hard (for others) to define. The lone wolf inclination has exhibited itself not only in her cultural pursuits, but also in foreign policy, in solutions to internal divisions, in accommodation and reactions to outsiders, and in the changing structures of her economic activities. The Finns' ability to devise their own remedies for threats to their national interest is an ongoing phenomenon. In political, commercial, industrial, and aesthetic spheres, Finnish formulas—different from those of neighbors, allies, and enemies—have inevitably surfaced and been applied frequently, more often than not with success.

The Dawn of the Historical Era

Finland's prehistoric period, in the centuries that followed the northerly advance of the early hunter-gatherers up to the "second wave" of immigrants who crossed the Baltic from Estonia around the time of the birth of Christ, is poorly documented. Archeological findings are scanty because of severe erosion and water logging, and the absence of farming activity due to the poorness of the topsoil deprived the area of the artifacts and other cultural clues that typify the Stone Age and Bronze Age of more southerly areas.

There was little unity among the early inhabitants of the Finnish land. For thousands of years tribes vied with each other for power and territory. Karelians dominated eastern areas while Tavastians, with their different language and culture, occupied central parts. The Finns proper clung to the coastal areas along the Gulf of Finland and up the Gulf of Bothnia and were more susceptible to Western influences coming from the south and west.

Regional differences notwithstanding, all the area's inhabitants, including the more recent arrivals, spoke a Uralic tongue, now referred to more commonly as belonging to the Finno-Ugrian group. Prior to the Swedish crusades in the twelfth century, the Swedish language (or any other Indo-European language) had no footing in the Finnish lands. Up to the twelfth century there was no Finnish state, merely a land where a cultural group (or groups) had found a way of making a living and which they had defended for centuries.

Sweden showed little political or military strength before the eleventh century, and it is feasible that the Finns, who often raided Swedish territory, were the stronger of the two entities. The Finnish language was spoken in parts of northern Sweden (as it still is today). But by the beginning of the twelfth century, Sweden was on the verge of developing into a formidable mediaeval power.

Between East and West

The watery, forested land between Ladoga and the Gulf of Bothnia represented in the twelfth century a kind of power vacuum, which vigorous neighbors to the east and west began to aim at and exploit. Viking expeditions from A.D. 800 onward had traveled the length of the Gulf of Finland and penetrated what is now Russia, often as far as the Black Sea. Finns—people living on Finnish territory—were gradually involved in such advances. The Vikings ruled Novgorod (in Russia) in 862 and Kiev a few years later. Because of Russia's growing power, it began to show an increasing interest in the land immediately to the west. There were religious (Orthodox) connections with the people there, and trading was common. According to the principles of the balance of power, it was natural that the now ambitious Swedes would covet the same territory. Thus, Finns in the early part of the twelfth century found themselves in the middle of a great power conflict, a situation that would persist—in hot and cold war periods—right up to 1945. The manner in which the Finns have dealt with this geopolitical balancing act defines to a large degree the history of the nation.

Finland—Province of the Kingdom of Sweden

The first Swedish military expedition, referred to as the First Crusade, took place in 1155. The foothold the Swedes gained on the southwest coast was too precarious to hold; the adventure ended in failure. In 1238 the Second Crusade was launched, which penetrated farther inland to Häme. The Third Crusade in 1293 reached the end of the Gulf of Finland, Viipuri (Viborg), where the Swedes built a fortress that still stands. The Russians in Novgorod, alarmed at the Swedish incursions, advanced from the east into Karelia. The Swedes, showing greater cohesion at the time, "won the race for Finland." The Treaty of Pähkinäsaari in 1323 defined Finland's eastern border clearly for the first time; it had been a moveable frontier for most of the thirteenth century. The 1323 border held for more than six hundred years, though it was crossed and recrossed during various periods of warfare. The Swedish advance to Viborg had, in effect, secured the future of Finland's development within the sphere of West European culture, though the Russo-Byzantine culture left its imprint on the eastern parts of the land.

Although Finland became a province of the Kingdom of Sweden, it was not occupied or subjugated. Rather, the Finns were partners in a shared nation. The growing number of Swedish settlements in Ostrobothnia and Uusimaa created, side-by-side with Finnish-speaking peasants, a unified, bilingual, Western Finnish culture. The second factor that anchored Finland firmly in the Western cultural domain was the advent of Christianity. The Christian religion, spreading east from Sweden, was brought to Finland by Bishop Henry of England. Turku Cathedral, which ranks number one among Finnish houses of worship, is more than seven hundred years old. Throughout the Middle Ages, for a period of 370 years, the Finns belonged to the Roman Catholic Church. Many eastern Finns adhered to the Orthodox religion. Uspenski Cathedral (Orthodox) dominates the Helsinki waterfront today. With the Reformation, Finns converted to Lutheranism.

The Swedish province of Finland became a political and administrative reality, with its two religions and two languages. Finns from Turku to Ladoga were Swedish subjects, and the capital of Finland was Stockholm. But Finns were not Swedes; neither were they oppressed. In 1362 Finns were granted the right to take part in the election of the Swedish king, and they sent representatives to the Diet. It is an interesting feature of Finnish history that during their adherence to both the Swedish and, later, Russian empires, the Finns have been treated with great respect by both sides. Finnish administrators, public figures, and military personnel were often openly coveted by the rulers of both Sweden and Russia. Both neighbors sought Finnish loyalty and allegiance. In fact the "Finnish card" has, throughout history, usually been a valuable one to play. During their checkered history, the Finns have skillfully exploited this neighborly respect. The Finnish card is played in international politics, even today: certain small nations cannot be treated lightly, as great powers such as Russia and the U.S. have discovered to their cost.

During the fourteenth century, life in western Finland resembled the Swedish model more than it did the eastern Finnish districts. Swedish law and a Scandinavian social system were established in Finland, and Finns enjoyed full political rights within the kingdom. The increasing political stability provided by these measures was in contrast to the situation in the eastern part of the country, where the semi-nomadic life and slash-and-burn agriculture of Savo and parts of Karelia led to an ill-defined national border, which Novgorod constantly tried to push westward. In the end the Swedes benefited from the nebulous nature of the eastern boundary lines by confirming, at the Treaty of Täyssinä in 1595, that the national border be fixed east of the Savo settlements and run to the Arctic Ocean by prolongation. Finland thus became a substantial territory in European terms (fifth-largest country in spite of its proximity to a giant and often expansive neighbor).

At the end of the Middle Ages, Finland's population, mostly consisting of small farmers, had topped 350,000. During this period of Swedish prosperity, Finnish life was relatively stable. It was not, however, peaceful. Sweden began to pay the cost of being a great power: Finnish manpower was needed for her armies, wars with Russia were constant, and Finnish territory was overrun twice by the Russians in 1710–1721 and 1741–1743. On each occasion the occupied land reverted to Sweden, but in a sense the writing was on the wall (and it was in Cyrillic script). A severe famine just before the beginning of the eighteenth century killed off nearly 30 percent of the Finnish population, and Sweden's grip on her eastern province weakened.

The completion of St. Petersburg in 1703 meant that the biggest city in Northern Europe had been built on Finnish land among Finnish-speaking people. The geographical position of the city was precarious in Russian eyes as long as Sweden remained powerful. As the eighteenth century progressed and Finland's population approached one million, the strategic value of the Karelian isthmus and its inhabitants became more apparent, especially as Sweden's days as a great power appeared numbered. In 1808 Russia took a decisive step and invaded Sweden's "Eastland" province—Finland. The Peace Treaty of Hamina in 1809 awarded the whole of Finland to Russia. Six hundred fifty years of Swedish rule came to an end.

Finland—Russian Grand Duchy

The period of Russian rule in Finland, which lasted 108 years (1809–1917), bore no resemblance in character or essence to other Russian occupations in the nineteenth and twentieth centuries. Once more, there had to be a Finnish formula—one that was acceptable to the czar but that, first and foremost, met the political and cultural requirements of the stubborn Finnish people. The first confirmation of a guarantee of dignity was apparent in Finland's status within the Empire. Finland was called a Grand Duchy (the Czar of Russia being also the Grand Duke of Finland) and was represented by a governor-general—a mechanism not unlike that between the King of England and Australia or Canada.

The czar, Alexander I, who had come to an agreement with Napoleon regarding Russia's interest in Finland, was a confirmed liberal. He treated the Finns and their Scandinavian institutions with due respect. Swedish laws remained in force, the Lutheran Church was left untouched, and all the members of the senate were Finns. They reported directly to the czar and were not responsible to the Russian Civil Service.

Alexander had his own requirements, but these were concerned primarily with defense. A major aim of Russian military policy was to move the first line of defense to the mouth of the Gulf of Finland, well away from St. Petersburg. This strategy was facilitated by Russia's access to the Åland Islands, giving Alexander a new western border only fifty miles off the Swedish coast. The czars built one of the biggest post offices in the world at Eckerö (the westernmost point of the Åland Islands) to serve as Russia's first face to the West. The building resembles Buckingham Palace in miniature.

The Finnish capital was also moved from Turku to Helsinki. Moving the seat of government further from Sweden yet still at a reasonable distance of comfort from Russia in effect strengthened the Finnish sense of national identity.

Alexander I died in 1825, and his successor, Nicholas I, was less liberal. He was careful, however, not to tamper with Finnish autonomy, and during his reign Finland became markedly more nationalistic.

Elias Lönnrot published the Finnish national epic poem, the *Kalevala,* in 1835, and J. L. Runeberg (who wrote in Swedish) came out with a series of patriotic poems. Both the *Kalevala* and Runeberg's poetry painted a picture of an idealized and romanticized Finnish countryside, mythical for sure, but instrumental in bringing to the attention of the educated classes of Europe the emergence of a distinctly Finnish (and not Scandinavian or Slavic) folkloric tradition.

This cultural impetus, along with the establishment of a separate Finnish currency (the *markka*) in 1860 and a conscript Finnish army in 1878, signaled advances in the momentum leading up to a modern Finnish state. Even periods of "Russification" by a less liberal czar, Nicholas II, from 1899 to 1905 and again from 1909 to 1917, could not stop this momentum.

When the Finns enacted a new constitution in 1906 and formed a single-chamber parliament with universal suffrage, replacing the old Four-Estates Diet, Finland with one stroke changed over from the oldest parliamentary system in Europe to the most modern; for example, Finnish women were the first on the continent to be given the vote. Another Finnish formula was coming into being; the writing was now on the wall for the Russians in terms of limited hegemony over the Finnish lands.

The Emerging Finnish State

To think of Finland as having lived under a Russian yoke from 1809–1917 is to make an inaccurate assessment of the Russo-Finnish relationship. The czars, at least Alexander I and Alexander II, took pains to appear no less benign regarding Finland than did Swedish monarchs.

In general the Finns responded by remaining loyal to Russia during the politically turbulent nineteenth century. Finnish was spoken on both sides of the border, reducing the confrontational aspect of the frontier. Thousands of Finns served in the Russian Imperial Army, four hundred of them actually achieving the rank of general or admiral. The partnership was geographically and politically viable—a situation that has always pleased Russian rulers as they pondered their western neighbor.

The nineteenth century, though an encouraging period for Finns, was, however, an uneasy time for Russia. Germany was growing rapidly in strength, and Russia's traditional nervousness about encirclement increased accordingly. The Russian government therefore strengthened the defenses of the Grand Duchy through the construction of fortifications and railways, but the increasing closeness of Finland's cultural ties with the West fanned Russian suspicions.

It is unlikely that the Finns, sharing administrative and military operations with Russia throughout the nineteenth century, envisioned their southern parts as a base for attack on Russia by a third power, but Russia never lost sight of this possibility. Indeed, this did eventually come to pass when Hitler launched his assault in 1940, though this was more than twenty years after Imperial Russia had passed into history.

In 1905 Russia suffered a severe military and psychological setback when the Japanese defeated the country in the Russo-Japanese War. This was the first occasion in modern times that an Asian power had vanquished a European one. This led to the czar acceding to the creation of a popular assembly in Russia, coinciding with the establishment of a Finnish single-chamber parliament. Although still not disloyal to the Russians, Finns had gradually been consolidating Finland's autonomy for over fifty years of Russian rule.

Alongside a democratically elected parliament, Finland also had most of the institutions of a modern state: a fiscal system (Bank of Finland), state railways, a separate legal system, an established church, a national currency, a coat of arms, a national anthem, two official languages, a university, a body of literature, its own newspapers, commercial companies, universal suffrage, and numerous societies and political associations. Imperial Russia, by contrast, had no viable parliament and a weak fiscal situation.

Finns remained loyal to Russia during the Crimean War and gave their eastern neighbor no reason to oppose them, thus furthering the development of a stronger sense of Finnish national identity. Alexander I had to some extent nurtured the concept of a separate Finnish culture, assuming (probably correctly) that it would distance Finns further from the Swedes and reduce the likelihood of Finland becoming a puppet of the West in the future.

Finland has historically demonstrated that she is nobody's puppet and has consistently followed a foreign policy that confined itself strictly to her own national interest. Even when she shared the German attack on the Soviet Union in 1940, Finland made it clear that she was not a German ally, but was only attempting to reclaim her own territory lost in the Winter War.

The Russians (and the Soviets) have frequently recognized this Finnish meticulousness concerning her military and political aims, and it stood her in good stead in the difficult days of the Cold War, when the Czechs and Hungarians took a beating at Russian hands. Kruschev, Molotov, and Brezhnev all exhibited reluctance to bully Finland, following an example set earlier by Lenin and Stalin. During the First World War Finnish industry supplied Russian materiel requirements, but the Bolshevik October Revolution of 1917 effected drastic changes in Russia and Europe. The Finns, loyal up to that point, saw their historical opportunity beckon and took it. Typically, pragmatism rather than ideology set the tone for the events that followed.

Independence

The first Russian Revolution, in March 1917, gave hope to liberal and progressive groups in Russia and was also favorable to Finnish interests, as there was no overwhelming desire among the Finnish public to break off relations completely with the Russian Empire. Occasional calls for complete Finnish autonomy or full independence had been mooted, and if the two periods of "Russification" (1899–1905 and 1909–1917, as mentioned earlier in the chapter) had not occurred, it is quite feasible that the Finns could have worked out a *modus vivendi* with Russia no less tolerable than the one they had shared with the Swedes for six centuries.

The Bolshevik Revolution in October, a few months later, changed everything, however. In that month the right-wing parties in the Finnish Parliament had a majority. Shocked and deeply worried by the gathering chaos in Russia, Parliament proclaimed itself the supreme authority in Finland on November 15, 1917, and appointed a new senate. Finns who had shown loyalty to the czars saw no reason to extend their loyalty to the restless mobs in Moscow and Leningrad. Hesitation was cast aside, and the typical Finnish propensity for swift and effective action came into play.

Nevertheless, even then, not all Finns wanted to break with Russia, and the Finnish Left rebelled. The presence of 70,000 Russian troops on Finnish land seemed to support the leftists' cause. But given the proud independent Finnish character and Finnish uneasiness with Russian troops on their soil, their presence in Finland turned out to be unfavorable for the Left. At all events, the Senate had to flee to Vaasa, and a civil war ensued.

The subsequent "Finnish formula" was the White Army, consisting largely of peasants and farmers, with a commander who had spent most of his military career in the Russian Imperial Army. This charismatic and formidable officer and statesman was Carl Gustav Emil Mannerheim, arguably the most imposing figure in Finnish history. This "White General," well acquainted with Winston Churchill and other influential figures in Britain and France, was asked by the Senate how long it would take him to beat the Red (Finnish) Army. His estimate of three months was accurate almost to the day, and he led the White Army down Helsinki's Esplanade in May 1918 to put the seal on Finland's middle-class victory—and independence.

Finland needed all Mannerheim's skill to extract her from what was a complex, delicate, and precarious political situation. Lenin had in fact recognized Finnish independence in December 1917, but Soviet troops were not withdrawn, and they went on to help the Reds in the Civil War.

In April 1918 a German division landed to take Helsinki. Germans, attempting to draw Finland into their sphere of influence, proposed a German prince be put on the Finnish throne. Prince Frederik Carl of Hessen was actually elected King of Finland. The Finns, desperately trying to keep on an even keel amidst the turmoil of Great Power politics, were greatly helped by Mannerheim's sangfroid and the propensity to keep a clean slate with the Allies. Not only was he pro-Anglo-Saxon, but he had also figured out that the Allies were going to win the war.

As it turned out, the calm course steered by the Finns was greatly steadied by military outcomes. Germany collapsed, so there would be no German monarch or alliance. The Bolsheviks ran rampant and the Empire, of which Finland had been a part, disintegrated. The new state was able, in its first decade, to foster relations with liberal and friendly countries: Estonia, Latvia, Lithuania, the Anglo-Saxons, and, of course, her Nordic neighbors. Finland became a member of the League of Nations, and her foreign and security policy remained relatively tranquil for two decades, until the rude shock in 1939.

Consolidating the State

In the 1920s and 1930s—the first twenty years of independence—the young republic took great strides forward, and the world at large witnessed, with some admiration, how Finns, with the freedom to do things their way, handled their affairs. An advantageous peace treaty with Russia was signed in 1920, giving Finland access to the Arctic Ocean with the ice-free port of Petsamo. Mannerheim, acting as regent after the Civil War, stayed at the helm from December 1918 until the summer of 1919, when Kaarlo Juho Ståhlberg was sworn in as the country's first president. In July 1919 Mannerheim ratified the Finnish constitution, which is still in force. The Finnish constitutional formula was a compromise between monarchist and republican objectives. Although one of their goals was democratic, parliamentary rule, the Finns, with one eye on the Americans, bestowed the office of president with sweeping powers and responsibility. Mannerheim, combining military leadership with outstanding statesmanship, had shown the value of a "strong man" at the helm. The Finnish constitution recognizes the president as commander-in-chief of the armed forces, allows him to dictate foreign policy, and gives him the right to dissolve Parliament. Both Ståhlberg and Lauri Kristian Relander, who followed him, did not hesitate to exercise this right.

Presidential power notwithstanding, Finnish governments have consistently demonstrated their adherence to democratic parliamentary rule. This was clearly indicated during the first presidency, when the Act of Amnesty was passed, pardoning the Civil War "Red" leaders and allowing the Social Democrats, who had in a sense lost the war, to take part in the subsequent elections. In fact this left-wing party formed a government from 1926 to 1927. The relative absence of vindictiveness in Finnish politics (in contrast to what happened elsewhere) continued throughout the 1920s and 1930s. For example, the ultra-right Lapuaists, who staged an anti-communist uprising in 1932, were defeated by the government without bloodshed.

Finland's focus during the 1920s was largely on the consolidation of national identity and the country's growing contribution to international intercourse. This was greatly aided by Finnish successes in sports, particularly the Olympic Games, where athletes such as Paavo Nurmi, Hannes Kolehmainen, and Ville Ritola "ran Finland onto the map of the world." In the 1936 Games, for instance, Finland was third, after the U.S. and Germany, and was due to stage the Olympic Games in Helsinki in 1940, had they not been cancelled on account of the war. Finnish victories in track events were repeated in the 1970s when Lasse Virén won both the 5,000, and 10,000-meter events in Munich and then again in Montreal. This modest four-time gold medalist is, at the time of writing, a Conservative in the Finnish Parliament.

The 1920s saw the introduction of compulsory education and conscriptive military service. Female voting strength led to the Prohibition Act, but because of Finland's cold climate, this law lasted only twelve years, and was repealed in 1932. Clubs, societies, and associations (the trappings of liberal states) multiplied, and a new body of Finnish literature made its appearance. Frans Emil Sillanpää won the Nobel Prize for Literature in 1939; Artturi Ilmari Virtanen for Chemistry in 1945; and Ragnar Granit for Medicine in 1967.

From 1920 onward Finland's cultural scene expanded and attracted international attention. The national ballet was founded as an extension of the Finnish opera in 1921. Theatrical performances flourished in both Swedish and Finnish. Jean Sibelius (1865–1957) became a world figure in music in the years leading up to World War II and was particularly lauded in the U.S., Britain, and Finland herself, where his swishing, boisterous, sometimes melancholy symphonies were seen as symbols of the national soul and of sturdy independence. Eliel Saarinen (1873–1950) enjoyed a worldwide reputation as an architectural genius both in Finland and the United States. His work, on both sides of the Atlantic, was repeated by two later Finnish internationally known architects, Alvar Aalto (1898–1976) and Viljo Revell (1910–1964).

Finnish painters, flocking to Paris during the late nineteenth and early twentieth centuries, succeeded in merging national and international styles. The best known were Eero Järnefelt and Albert Edelfelt, who launched Finnish impressionism, and Akseli Gallen-Kallela (1865–1931), who put the national epic *Kalevala* on canvas and gave the world a visual image of the mythical land of Lönnrot's poetic collection.

By the 1930s, Finnish leaders in the fields of diplomacy, business, and artistic activity were traveling abroad and making other countries, particularly in Europe and North America, aware of their energy and talent. By 1939, culturally speaking, Finland "had arrived."

The Winter War

The Finnish rapprochement with the Scandinavian and Anglo-Saxon countries was in clear conformity with the inclinations of the Finnish people, who were already enjoying the fruits of democracy, liberalism, and recognition by Western civilization. In the end, though, she paid for her dallying dearly, as traditional Russian suspicion came to a head. Democracies are often so convinced of the rightness of their course that they are slow to perceive that they are in danger from less democratic neighbors. The Czechs fell victim to Hitler in 1938, and the Low Countries (Netherlands, Belgium, and Luxemburg), as well as Denmark and Norway, were next on the list.

Mannerheim and the president at that time, J. K. Paasikivi, experienced statesmen both, were well aware that the Russians would counter German expansion. When the Soviets, in 1938 and 1939, offered Finland large tracts of land in Karelia in exchange for the southern parts of the Karelian Isthmus, both men suggested serious consideration of this offer as the least onerous of various alternatives. The Finnish government, with one eye on its Western contacts and the other contemplating the fate of the Baltic States, took the tough line and declined negotiations.

The Soviets attacked in November 1939, and the Finns, though defending tenaciously and inflicting enormous losses on the Russian troops, had to sue for peace after only three months. The Russians took the land they wanted, gaining 10 percent of Finnish territory. Finland learned the lesson that in war she had to go it alone and that she lived next door to a neighbor she was unlikely ever to vanquish. Consequently, her policy in the future was to tread very carefully on Russian soil, even when she invaded it. This in itself is a tightrope act that the West did not fully understand in the years 1940–1990.

The Continuation War

When Hitler attacked the Soviet Union in June of 1941, Finland declared herself neutral. It was a temporary, almost symbolic ploy, for it was clear she must choose one side or the other—or suffer occupation. When the Soviets bombed several Finnish cities, the choice was made for her. In any case, no other route was open. German troops were moving through Sweden and Finland, and besides, the Finns had land to reclaim. The Finnish army launched a "separate" attack and shortly thereafter crossed the old Russo-Finnish border and fought on Russian soil.

Their strategy was carefully thought out; they wanted neither to participate in the German siege of Leningrad nor to break Leningrad's supply line to the Arctic Ocean. Russian land taken by the Finns was understood to be potential territory for exchange in making the inevitable peace. Mannerheim, once more in charge, followed a strict Finnish agenda, which, after the German collapse at Stalingrad, became all the more clear. When the Russians asked Finland to drive out the Germans, Mannerheim did not hesitate. He saw this as an escape route from Russian occupation and an additional favor Finland could grant the Allies, who would dictate peace terms and with whom Mannerheim envisaged comfortable relations in the postwar period.

And that is how it turned out. Eventually, Finland rid herself of the German connection, unloaded the Russians (after paying war reparations), and finished with a clean sheet with the Anglo-Saxons and Western democracies. As for the Nordic countries, one can assume they were grateful to the Finns and the Finnish army. As Finns are wont to say, "We did not win the war, but we came second." But that was later. Hard times came first.

Licking the Wounds

At the truce of September 1944, Finland was war-battered, wounded, fragile, and imposed upon. Desperate to stay out of the Great Power conflict, she had ended up conducting hostilities against both sides. The Germans had razed Lapland to the ground on their way out, the Russians were hammering on the back door for war reparations, and 420,000 Karelians were streaming across the border needing shelter, land, and a means of conducting a livelihood.

Finland had been truly unlucky. As Hitler and Stalin wreaked havoc with the continent, Finland, like the Baltic States and Poland, had been directly in the firing line. She had, however, been more nimble. Though having to cede 10 percent of her eastern territory and losing her Arctic outlet in Petsamo, she had side-stepped, at least temporarily, the issue of her sovereignty and did not have to suffer the indignity of a Soviet-controlled communist government running her affairs (as was the case in Estonia, Latvia, Lithuania, and Poland, not to mention other Soviet satellites further south).

From 1945 onward, Finns, with Mannerheim again president,

controlled Finnish destiny. The Soviet Union, herself war-battered, was not in a position to force Finland to accept a puppet government. The Finnish army had never been routed, plus a Russian occupation of 337,000 square kilometers of chilly territory (winter was beginning) would have been a costly and internationally unpopular affair.

Mannerheim was experienced, cool, and calculating. When the Americans offered Marshall Plan aid to Finland, he showed his nimbleness by refusing it. It would have been useful to help pay off war debts, but hardship is often the price of independence. The Finnish people as a whole have always shown themselves willing to pay this price. What other country ever paid off its war debts? Britain and the U.S., in particular, were impressed as Finland balanced her books with the Soviets.

In an era when refugee problems often dragged on for decades, Finland absorbed her 420,000 Karelians with a minimum of fuss and fluster. They were Finnish citizens who had turned down the offer of a Russian passport: how else could they be treated other than with fairness and justice? It was another notch in Finnish achievement, though it also meant the tightening of the national belt another notch.

The war reparations were paid off by 1952 when the Olympic Games were held in Helsinki. Though an onerous undertaking, paying their war debt to Russia turned out to be ultimately beneficial to the Finnish nation, because the new industries that had to be set up to supply the products the Russians insisted upon flourished in the following decade. The Soviets, at first tough creditors, became dependent on Finnish products, a situation that has continued into the twenty-first century. These products—a good fit for the requirements of Russian industry—sell at market prices.

The wars with the Soviets had cost Finland dearly: 65,000 dead and 158,000 wounded. The small Nordic countries such as Finland cannot afford such losses. Each one, by a different route, eventually sought accommodation with its giant northern neighbor. Mannerheim and then Paasikivi were able to convince the Soviets in

1944–1948 that it was in Russia's best interest for Finland to maintain its defense forces at acceptable strength. The formula was, as usual, elegant: Finland must be strong enough to resist her use as a base for attack (on Russia or anybody else) by a third party. This was confirmed by the signing of a Treaty on Friendship, Cooperation and Mutual Assistance in 1948. Finnish commitments in this treaty, which in Finland became known as the Paasikivi Line, led German politicians to coin the phrase "Finnlandisierung" or "Finlandization," implying Finnish submission to Russian demands.

It was widely assumed in Western countries (by many people who should have known better) that Finns had suffered the same indignities and lack of freedoms as the Poles, Czechs, Estonians, and others had. It was not at all clear, even for educated Western Europeans, on which side of the Iron Curtain Finland was standing. Yet only one day on Finnish soil would have made it evident to any visitor that life in postwar Finland resembled strongly that in Sweden or Norway or Denmark and bore almost no similarity to that of Eastern European countries. The 1948 treaty, though appearing sinister to some, was certainly a preferable formula, considering what happened to Czechoslovakia in that year. In the most hazardous period of the Cold War, Finland proved that it was possible to maintain friendly relations with the Soviet Union while simultaneously strengthening her political, economic, and cultural ties with the West, particularly, but not only, with her Nordic neighbors.

Down the Back Straight

The second half of the twentieth century was kinder to Finland than the first. The 1952 Olympic Games showed Finland's face to the world; it had Western features. Finns from all walks of life ventured abroad in increasing numbers and rapidly became more visible internationally. President Paasikivi (1946–1956) and his durable successor, Urho Kekkonen (in office 1956–1982), kept things on an even keel with Messrs. Malenkov, Kosygin, Khruschev, and Brezhnev.

Finland joined the Nordic Council, an interparliamentary body, was accepted into the United Nations in 1955, and joined EFTA (the European Free Trade Association) in 1961. In 1973 she concluded a comprehensive customs agreement with the European Economic Community (EEC) and nimbly made a similar agreement with the Eastern bloc's COMECON in the same year.

In 1989 Finland became a member of the Council of Europe. It was only a matter of time before membership in the European Union was offered, and Finns, showing less hesitation than the Swedes, voted the country in by referendum in 1995. The simultaneous accession of Finland and Sweden to the EU gave the Union an extra northern dimension in addition to that provided by Britain, Denmark, and Germany. This not only subtly changed the way in which the committees functioned but also provided the EU with a common frontier with Russia. Finnish delegations dealing with that country represent EU interests as well as their own.

EU members also feel that almost two centuries of direct contact with Russians have given Finns special expertise in negotiating with them. Certainly Finland's geographical position and the eastern-western-northern elements in her cultural history lend credence to the idea that Finns are ideal mediators between the EU, Russia, and the Baltic States. The Finns have not shunned this role and, during their successful 1999 EU presidency, demonstrated their evenhandedness and growing competence in the international arena. The usefulness of Finland's constructive and active neutrality was recognized by thirty-five countries in the Helsinki Agreement of 1975 at the European Conference on Security and Cooperation in Europe.

The full extent of modern Finland's involvement in international linkages can be seen in the number of organizations she belongs to and is active in. These include, in addition to the EU and the Nordic Council, the OSCE, the Council of Europe (as mentioned earlier), the Council of Baltic Sea States, the Arctic Council, the Barents Euro-Arctic Council, and the Euro-Atlantic Partnership Council. Though not a full member of NATO, Finland was an observer at the North Atlantic Cooperation Council in 1992 and has belonged to the NATO Partnership for Peace since 1994.

The progression from Arctic survivor to Sweden's eastern province to Tsarist Grand Duchy to independence through three wars and finally to the EU haven was long, arduous, and often lonely. Serving as the EU president at the end of the twentieth century would have seemed an unlikely prospect at the end of the nineteenth century. It is comforting to friends of Finland to see that her stamina, steadfastness, honesty, and undeniable reserves of talent have finally paid off.

THE UNIQUE
FINNISH LANGUAGE

Finnish is one of around twenty Uralic languages still spoken over a vast territory stretching from the Baltic Sea and Arctic Ocean in the west over the Ural Mountains and beyond the banks of the Siberian river Ob in the northeast. The Votyak, Mari, and Mordvin members of the family, spreading along the southern Urals, look southwest to the southernmost speakers of the Uralic tongue, Hungarians. Thus the Uralic languages almost complete a great linguistic circle around the Slavic heart of European Russia (see Figure 5.1). Proto-Uralic may have had a much wider playground, reaching as far west as the British Isles.

What is the source of the vitality and resilience of this linguistic strain that has defied the almost unstoppable march of the forty Indo-European languages as well as a millennium of pressure from Turkic languages on its southern flank? How have such small cultural pockets such as the Lapps (35,000) and the Ostyaks (15,000) fended off assimilation by much heftier neighboring cultural groups? What is so special about Uralic tongues, and Finnish in particular, and what do these languages sound like? An English speaker

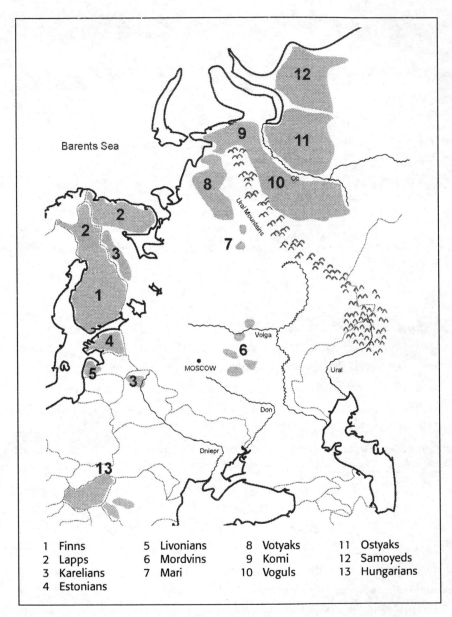

FIGURE 5.1   Uralic Encirclement of European Russia

visiting Finland for the first time (on a boat going from Stockholm to Helsinki) volunteered the following description:

> All around me I was hearing the Finnish language (*suomea*) for the first time—a gripping experience for a sound-hungry linguist. Its abundance of vowels and flowing liquidity at first remind one of Italian or Polynesian, but, as one listens, one detects underlying, vibrant sinews unheard in southern tongues, yet quite unlike tough, thrusting Germanic. The impressive length of its regimented nouns and adjectives, the musicality of its coordinated case endings, the rippling sonority of its convoluted sentences, all hint at the artistic, tenacious soul of a people come from afar. The language has in it the swishing coniferous forests and boisterous Arctic streams that we hear in the music of Sibelius, the loneliness and cold melancholy of the northern lakes, the unlimited, invigorating roaming of the Central Asian steppes, the vitality and perseverance of adventurous, hardened, migrant explorers. I sat and listened in awe, understanding not a word, but completely captivated by the unfaltering harmonics of this nimble Asian tongue. For me it was more entertaining than any symphony.

Uralic Language Structure

It is evident that the English speaker we have quoted was greatly moved by the sounds of Finnish. At the same time, he was listening to a multiplicity of Uralic language structures, though he was not able to decipher them at that point. What are these durable structures of these languages, inherent in Proto-Uralic and surviving in modern Finnish, Estonian, and Lappish? A speaker of Indo-European languages (English, Russian, German, etc.), on studying Finnish, encounters an abundance of unfamiliar forms, structures, and concepts of language absent from Latin, Greek, and Germanic or Slavic

TABLE 5.1   The Finnish Noun Table

	Singular	*Plural*
Nominative	talo	talot
Genitive	talon	talojen
Essive	talona	taloina
Partitive	taloa	taloja
Translative	taloksi	taloiksi
Inessive	talossa	taloissa
Elative	talosta	taloista
Illative	taloon	taloihin
Adessive	talolla	taloilla
Ablative	talolta	taloilta
Allative	talolle	taloille
Abessive	talotta	taloitta
Comitative	–	taloineen
Instructive	–	taloin

(The singular forms of the **Comitative** and **Instructive** are not in common use.)

tongues. Modern Finnish has remained relatively faithful to ancient Proto-Uralic inasmuch as it has retained many features that are common to most existing Uralic languages. The most striking is the complex declension of the noun, which takes fourteen case endings in Finnish (Uralic average, twelve). This is set out in Table 5.1, above.

Other characteristics of Finnish structure shared with the majority of Uralic languages (and uncommon in Indo-European) can be listed as follows:

- **No gender:** Nouns are not classified as masculine, feminine, or neuter as in many Indo-European languages (though not English). In Finnish there is only one word for *he* and *she* (*hän*).
- **No definite or indefinite articles:** *Talo* means "house," "the house," or "a house."

- **Stress on first syllable of all words:** Hélsinki, Róvaniemi, *tálossannekin, sánomalehtitoimisto,* etc.
- **Large number of vowels:** Finnish has 8 (*a, e, i, o, u, ä, ö, y*), and the Uralic average is 10.
- **Few consonants:** Finnish has only 13 consonants in a 21-letter alphabet. *B, c, f, q, w, x,* and *z* do not exist in Finnish unless they appear in foreign loan words.
- **No verb "to have":** In place of a verb "to have," the Uralic languages use the verb "be." They express the agent (possessor) by a dative or locative case; for example, in Finnish:

  isä: father   *on:* is   *talo:* house

  isällä on talo: "father has a house" (literally "to father is house")
- **No prepositions:** Prefixes and prepositions were unknown in Proto-Uralic. Although modern Finnish has developed some prepositions (e.g., *ilman:* "without"), this was due largely to Germanic influence. The declension system routinely obviates the use of prepositions in Finnish:

talo	house
talotta	without a house
talossa	in the house
taloon	to the house
talosta	from the house
- **Compound nouns:** The formation of nouns in Proto-Uralic included compounding two, three, or more words. This is a striking feature of modern Finnish, where many words achieve an impressive length; for example:

talo	house
ryhmä	group
taloryhmä	group of houses
sanoma	word
lehti	leaf (page)
toimisto	place of activity
sanomalehtitoimisto	press office

- **Conjugation:** Uralic verbs exhibit some unfamiliar (and some familiar) peculiarities for Indo-Europeans. Conjugation in Finnish is familiar to students of Latin-based languages:

ostan	I buy
ostat	you (familiar) buy
hän ostaa	he/she buys
ostamme	we buy
ostatte	you buy
he ostavat	they buy

- **Changeable negative markers:** Unlike fixed Indo-European negative markers such as *nicht, inte, ikke, non, no, ne . . . pas*, and so forth, Finnish has changeable markers:

puhun	I speak	*en puhu*	I don't speak
puhut	you speak	*et puhu*	you don't speak
hän puhuu	he speaks	*hän ei puhu*	he doesn't speak
puhumme	we speak	*emme puhu*	we don't speak
puhutte	you speak	*ette puhu*	you don't speak
he puhuvat	they speak	*he eivät puhu*	they don't speak

- **Interrogatives:** In Proto-Uralic, questions were formed with interrogative pronouns beginning with *k-*. This system lives on in Finnish (*kuka:* who? *kenen:* whose?).
- **Yes/no questions:** These are asked in Finnish by attaching to the verb the interrogative particles *ko* and *kö:*

tulet You are coming	*tuletko?* Are you coming?
menen I am going	*menenkö?* Am I going?

  Interestingly, Japanese asks questions by attaching *ka* to the verb:

kimasu He is coming	*kimasu-ka?* Is he coming?

- **Richness of verbal derivation:** Verbal derivation was already richly developed in Proto-Uralic. Finnish abounds in such constructions: four different infinitives, a host of participles, and verbal nouns and adjectives. All these can be declined fourteen different ways—fun for an ardent linguist!

If all these considerations make Finnish appear difficult for an Indo-European learner, it only confirms the fact that one does not easily learn a language that differs wildly in structure and thought processes from one's own. Yet Finnish children learn Finnish effortlessly, so grammar is mainly in one's (a foreigner's) mind!

Finnish is what the Americans call a "fun" language. The intricate and disciplined morphology presents a wonderful challenge to the motivated learner. The musicality provided by vowel harmony and noun-adjective case agreement (*toisella hyvällä paikalla*) give the non-Finn great satisfaction as he or she reels them off the tongue. The very strangeness of the Uralic vocabulary has an exotic flavor. Some sentences, too, have a soft charm and lilt: *Aja hiljaa sillalla.* ("Drive slowly over the bridge.") Even the basic Uralic numbers have a refreshing sharpness to them: (1) *yksi*, (2) *kaksi*, (3) *kolme*, (4) *neljä*, (5) *viisi*, (6) *kuusi*, (7) *seitsemän*, (8) *kahdeksan*, (9) *yhdeksän*, (10) *kymmenen*.

Analysis, Synthesis, and Depth of Thought

Sanskrit, Greek, and Latin were all highly flexional, that is to say, they used case endings extensively and built up a descriptive grammatical system suited to this type of language. Over the last five hundred years, however, most Indo-European languages, particularly English, have discarded their flexional endings and evolved an "analytical" system of position and prepositions where meaning is conveyed by a series of "shortish" words in a strict word order. Modern Chinese, too, follows this pattern. Some Indo-European languages like Russian, Lithuanian, Latvian, and, to a lesser extent, German, have retained some of their case endings.

Other non-Indo-European languages such as Finnish, Turkish, and Hungarian have a far greater number of cases (Finnish has fourteen) so that the word order and train of thought involved differs greatly from that of the "analytical" French or English speaker. To an English speaker, German appears difficult, Turkish complex, and Finnish probably very complex.

If we take Finnish as an extreme example with its fourteen cases and innumerable participles and suffixes, there are grounds for believing that Finns think more deeply than others, simply by enjoying more variety of self-expression as they utilize "complex" mechanisms that we do not possess. Finnish words tend to contain several elements that would require several words in English, though they are usually longer than ours. A Finn would often seem therefore to enjoy economy of expression, fitting different factors neatly into one or two words, when we would "rabbit on."

Let us take a few examples:

asun	I live
talo	house
talossa	in the house
talonne	your house
talossanne	in your house
-kin	also
asun talossannekin	I live in your house, too!
lähteä	to leave
lähtisi	ought to leave
-mme	we
-kö	interrogative marker
hän	for emphasis
lähtisimmeköhän!	I wonder whether we ought to go or not.

tulla	come
tultua	having come
-mme	we
-kaan	not even
tultuammekaan	not even after we had arrived

On the day Princess Grace of Monaco was killed, the headline in *Iltasanomat* read "*Grace Kolarista Sairaalaan.*" The use of case endings economized on what would have been in English: "Immediately after the accident Grace was taken straight to the hospital."

The Lapps also deal in lengthy one-word concepts. In 1981 a Lapland bar owner failed in his attempt to register the name "Santos" for his establishment. In a fit of fury he dredged up a Lappish place name, and his bar was duly registered (without opposition) as *Ateritsiputeritsipuolilautatsi Baari.*

Apart from the intriguing nature of long, pregnant-with-meaning words in Finnish, it is the elaborate case system that largely contributes to its richness. Using a language with fourteen to fifteen cases means you can do virtually anything with a noun, and with a huge selection of verb-participles also declining like nouns, there are endless permutations. As the case endings clearly indicate the function of the noun, adjective, or declined participle, the meaning is clear regardless of word order.

This means that the Finn can play around with word order for emphasis, nuance, or other desired effect, whereas the English or Chinese speaker is denied this luxury, except in language of poetic or literary character. Finns, with their multiplicity of prefixes, suffixes, and inserted plural markers, as well as numerous infinitive and participle forms all declining fourteen different ways, have an enormous number of linguistic tools and devices at their disposal. This facilitates great flexibility and variation of expression. Also, in terms of vocabulary, the Finno-Ugrian languages are extremely rich in total number of words and variant forms.

What we refer to as "complex" languages are often (1) "agglutinative" tongues (Finnish, Hungarian, Turkish), where concept length is attained by gluing elements together, or (2) "polysynthetic" languages such as Basque or many Amerindian dialects, where an entire series of concepts such as "I am looking for two of the enemy" is contained within a single word. The speakers of these languages are not aware of thinking in a more complicated manner than we do, although the dense, synthetic build-up spoken at speed bewilders the Indo-European learner (with his or her "analytical" train of thought).

These considerations are set out to show that as we leave the Indo-European field we encounter vast and fundamental differences in linguistic mentality. Although all human languages evolve along parallel thought-and-language processes to some extent, the more remote a language is from our own, the more diverse is the thought. Polysynthetic Basque, with its *ponetekilakoarekin* (the one who has the cap), shows an opaqueness that is matched by the Amerindian (Oneida) *gnaglaslizaks* (I am looking for a village). Finnish *tultuammekaan* (not even after we had arrived) is right in this class.

Benjamin Whorf believed that one's segments of experience were limited by the vocabulary and concepts inherent in one's language. By learning more languages, especially those with excitingly different concepts, one could widen one's vision and gain deeper insight into the nature of reality. Many graduates in Romance studies feel enriched by being able to see the world through Spanish eyes or by using French rationality. Scholars of Chinese or Japanese often develop two personalities when immersing themselves in one of these two languages. The study of the writing system accentuates this development. The Finnish language, with its rich vocabulary and multiplicity of unique structures, opens many new avenues of thought for those few foreigners who study it in depth.

FINNISH BELIEFS AND VALUES

Finns think their minds are free, but they have been thoroughly brainwashed. Collective programming in all cultures, begun in the cradle and reinforced in kindergarten, school, and workplace, convinces us that we are normal, others eccentric.

Geert Hofstede described culture as "the collective programming of the mind." Though not as sinister as the term brainwashing—with its connotations of political coercion—it nevertheless describes a process to which each one of us has been subjected from birth.

Finnish parents and teachers obviously give children the best advice they can. This programming fits them out for successful interaction in Finnish culture and society, where good and bad, right and wrong, normal and abnormal are clearly defined. Unfortunately (at least in one sense), children in other lands are being given a completely different set of instructions, though equally valid in their own environment.

These taught-and-learned "national" concepts become, as we grow up, our core beliefs, which we find almost impossible to discard. On the one hand, we regard others' beliefs and habits (Russian, Chinese, Arab) as strange or eccentric, mainly because they are unlike our own.

There is no doubt about it, Finns are not like Italians!

On the other hand, we have a sneaking feeling (and we frequently hear it expressed) that "deep down all people are alike." There is also truth in this, for there are such things as characteristics universal to humankind. They are not numerous, for our national collective programming distorts some of our basic instincts (Scottish thrift versus American free spending). Figure 6.1 shows how national collective programming is "grafted onto" inherited (human) traits. In the top section we add individual characteristics.

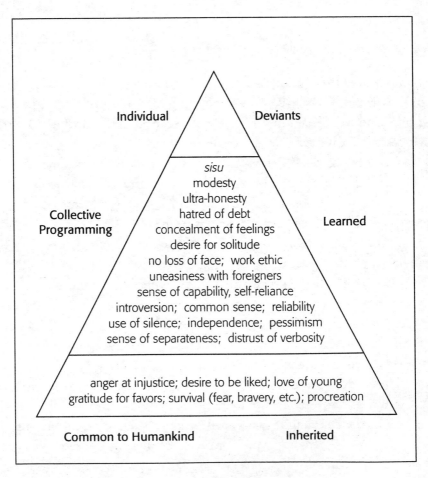

FIGURE 6.1   Finnish Human Mental Programming

Some people, by dint of personal originality, extra powers of perception, stubbornness, or even genius, stand apart from their fellows and deviate sharply from the national track. Such people often become famous for their "idiosyncrasies," and a few have actually changed the course of their nation's destiny (King Henry VIII, Kemal Atatürk, Emperor Meiji of Japan, President Kekkonen of Finland).

In general, however, our national or regional culture imposes itself upon our behavior rather than the other way round, and we become a solid German, a good Finn, a real American, or a true Brit, as the case may be. Interacting with our compatriots, we generally find that the closer we stick to the rules of our society, the more accepted and comfortable we become.

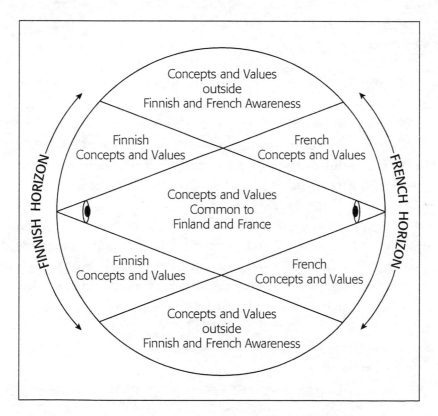

FIGURE 6.2   Finnish/French Horizons

Life within Horizons

Our genes, our parental and educational training, our societal rules, our very language, enable us to see as far as our horizon, and that is the limit. From our standpoint we cannot see *beyond* our horizon. We can *broaden* it to some degree by living in other countries, by learning foreign languages, and by reading books on philosophy, psychology, other cultures, and a variety of other subjects. The multicultural (I use this term in its international sense) person widens his or her horizon by these means. Unless we make such efforts, our horizon remains a British horizon, an American horizon, a Japanese horizon, or one of many other worldviews. In other words, each culture enjoys a certain segment of experience—one that is no more than a fraction of the total possible experience available to humankind.

Multicultural man or woman seeks to strive toward "totality of experience" (impossible to achieve in a lifetime) not only by learning foreign languages but by cultivating empathy with the views of others, standing in their shoes in their geographical, historical, and philosophical location, seeing himself or herself from that location and trying to fuse a multiplicity of beliefs, talents, skills, values, and vibrant, positive qualities into a viable, benign procedure toward a cosmopolitan understanding.

These are great ideals, obtainable only in the future, though the process has begun. For the moment, we live within our limited horizons. Figure 6.2, on the previous page, shows how Finns and the French, looking at the world from different standpoints, see some things in a similar light (sense of justice, work ethic, and democracy) while other concepts are visible only to one nationality. A third area, containing a variety of beliefs and philosophies, lies outside the ken of either Finns or the French.

Finnish Lutheran values are accepted unquestioningly at home, but they take a quick beating on foreign soil. For instance, the concept of truth is universal, but *notions* of that concept differ wildly.

Finnish truth is not Spanish truth, just as Chinese duty is not American duty, or British revenge not of the Sicilian variety. Truth, in the Finnish mind, is strict adherence to facts. Like Germans (*die Wahrheit ist die Wahrheit*), they believe that there is such a thing as scientific truth. Finns open and conduct meetings with the premise that stating the truth, whether pleasant or not, is the best way to achieve a successful outcome. They are astonished to find that only Germans, North Americans (Canadians and U.S. Americans), Norwegians, and Australians have the same attitude. Swedes almost make it into this category but shy away from truth if it is too unpleasant. The Danes and Dutch are more "devious" (in a pleasant way) than they look, while the British chairman's prime objective is "not to rock the boat." In Italy truth is negotiable, in France it is dressed up, the Spanish play with "double truth." Russians are compulsive liars (often for good reasons), in Japan truth is regarded as a dangerous concept, and in China there is no such thing as absolute truth: diametrically opposed things can both be true at the same time.

Mental and moral elasticity of this nature often confuses the Finn, who has been brought up in a world where trains and buses leave on time and where people pay their bills within twenty-four days, turn up punctually for appointments, and cross the road when the light is green. Finns are individualists, but in Finland individualism does not involve breaking the law or a promise, juggling with facts, or saying one thing when meaning another.

Contradictions and Paradoxes in the Finnish Mindset

Finns are warm-hearted people, but they have a desire for solitude. They are hard working and intelligent but often seem slow to react. They love freedom, but they curtail their own liberty by closing their shops early, limiting their access to alcohol, prohibiting late baths in apartment buildings, and taxing themselves to death. They worship athletics and fitness, but until recently their diet gave them the highest incidence of heart disease in Western Europe. They admire coolness and calm judgment but drink a bit too much. They are eager to internationalize but pretend they can't learn languages. They want to communicate but wallow in introversion. They make fine companions but love to brood alone by a lake. They are tolerant but secretly despise people who are melodramatic or appear to be overly emotional. They are essentially independent but often hesitate to speak their mind in the international arena (this led to the silly term "Finlandization," coined by people who did not really know them). They are genuinely democratic, but they often let the "tyranny of the majority" (a Japanese figure of speech) rule. They are fiercely individualistic but are at the same time afraid of "what the neighbors might say." They are Western in outlook but, like the Asians, cannot abide "losing face." They are resourceful but often portray themselves as hapless. They are capable of acting alone but frequently take refuge in group collusion. They desire to be liked but make no attempt to charm. They love their country but seldom speak well of it.

Ten Basic Finnish Values

Finnish values are strong inasmuch as they are shared by the nation, are rarely compromised or diluted, and are seen as a code of ethical behavior. The ten outstanding traits listed in this section are characteristic of Finnish *males*. Although Finnish women share all of them to some degree (except perhaps taciturnity), they differ from the men in style and nuance. The Finnish female mindset is dealt with more fully in Chapter 12.

Sense of Separateness

Finns feel a sense of separateness from other nationalities. They are not Scandinavians, they are not Slavs, and their distinctive language, as discussed in Chapter 5, is not even Indo-European. Though Estonians and Karelians are accepted as Finnic kin, the other Finno-Ugrian speakers, the Hungarians, are far off and barely relevant.

The Finnish people are tightly bonded in their sense of separateness not only by their unique language and culture, but also by their bleak, isolated geography, their struggle to survive, and their obsession to succeed when, in the past, they knew they stood alone.

The importance of the Finnish language as an irresistibly binding factor to those who wield it in shining separateness cannot be overestimated. One is left in no doubt as to the statement it makes: We, the Finns, live up here in the North with you neighbors. We may like you and get on well with you, but you see and hear that we are different. We have our own language and literature, folklore, artistry and aesthetics, music, and sense of shape and color—in short, a unique worldview.

The Finnish sense of separateness is accompanied by a high degree of national self-consciousness. It is a characteristic the Finns share with the Japanese, Chinese, and French, though they are less chauvinistic than these nationalities. Finns are very interested in cultural relativism—the way they differ from others. They discuss this subject at length, occasionally developing complexes that do not always correspond to reality. The question of the "Finnish difference" was once primarily in the realm of the arts, literature, and assertion of political independence. Today it raises its head in the development and conduct of international business.

Sisu

This most typical of Finnish values, *sisu,* often referred to by Finns, defies exact translation. The nearest English equivalent is "guts." Sisu implies courage, toughness, stamina, stubbornness, single-mindedness, and tenacity—the ability to endure hardship and adversity. When the world shrugged its shoulders at the inevitability of Finland's fate in 1939, sisu was the quality that enabled the Finns to survive against incredible odds. It also sustained them for an additional four years in the Continuation War against a state whose population was in excess of two hundred million. Finnish sisu was the bedrock under Mannerheim's boots as he negotiated the peace that guaranteed the country's independence. In the postwar period, sisu provided the stamina that enabled the nation to pay off crippling war reparations. It carried them through two periods of economic depression, engendered the energy to consolidate industrial and commercial advances in the 1970s and 1980s, and was rewarded by international recognition when Finland qualified for admittance to the European Union.

Honesty

Finns, like the Japanese and the Germans, think they are the most honest of all peoples. However, the concept of honesty varies considerably from culture to culture. Finnish honesty is of the blue-eyed, uncompromising, law-abiding variety, where truth is truth (the scientific kind). As discussed earlier in this chapter, deviousness is taboo, and people pay their taxes. One Finnish prime minister was dismissed the day after it was discovered that she had used a "terminological inexactitude" to Parliament, even though she was the leader of the majority party and had other sterling qualities that might have served the office well. It is unlikely this would have happened in the U.S., Italy, France, or any other country. On both political and economic fronts, Finns have a reputation for being straightforward players. Not only does this stand them in good stead in the EU, but it has frequently gained them points in their dealings with Russians at all levels.

Hatred of Debt

Finnish honesty is particularly noticeable when it comes to the abhorrence of indebtedness. Hatred of even minor debts makes Finns consistently query, at a personal level, if they owe you anything. I have seen a forest-dwelling acquaintance walk three miles in the snow to repay one *markka*. Finnish companies like to pay their bills within a month of receiving them. A recent European business survey shows they pay faster than any other country in the EU. At the government level, the compunction to remain out of debt is internationally acknowledged. The war reparations paid between 1945 and 1952 are only the best-known example. Finnish fiscal compliance with EU regulations has been exemplary.

Whence this hatred of debt? One can assume that its origin lies partly in the hardships of Finnish history. Debt-free status sits well with the spirit of fierce independence. One also pays less interest.

Luotettavuus

Finns judge you by your degree of *luotettavuus* (reliability). There must be a strong word-deed correlation when you are dealing with them. Do what you have said you are going to do. In Finland a statement can be regarded as a kind of promise (to be kept). Spaniards, Italians, and other exuberant people can get into trouble with Finns if they make euphoric plans and do not follow through with them.

Overt body language may also make Finns think you are unreliable, though this may not be the case. Luotettavuus is closely allied with a steady work ethic, enhanced by capability. Give a Finn a job and he or she will do it. Foreigners gain points with Finns by demonstrating their own competence. The main maxim is not to promise more than you can deliver.

Shyness and Modesty

Finns are basically shy, especially with foreigners, but also with others they do not know well. Modesty and humility, though not taken to the extreme lengths as in Japan or China, are nevertheless regarded as positive traits. It is no exaggeration to say that some Finns from country districts are obsessed with self-effacement. Privacy is important, and most Finns enjoy solitude from time to time. In Finland one minds one's own business; gossip is frowned upon. A recent survey of attitudes in fifty countries showed that the two categories of people who were least susceptible to flattery were Finnish and New Zealand males. Finnish modesty and shyness lead to an unwillingness to impose their will on others. Persistent persuasion—or worse, the hard sell—are prohibitory. One may recommend a product or course of action but should refrain from applying pressure if the other shows little inclination to accept.

Taciturnity

The first thing new arrivals in Finland are struck by is the taciturnity of Finnish males. The latter in turn are often put off by foreign loquacity and may react by retreating further into their shell. This can have quite a profound and often negative effect on extroverted people such as Latins, Arabs, and Africans, though Americans also find Finns a bit short of words. Basically, Finns distrust verbosity. If you speak for more than four or five minutes at a time, they begin to wonder what you are trying to hide. Finns say only what is necessary to explain a situation. Generally, they are very brief indeed. They are good summarizers. Finnish communication is dealt with more fully in the next chapter. Suffice it to say here that Finns do not tell you their feelings or all that is in their mind and are more comfortable being silent.

Directness

Though Finns prefer to speak briefly, when they do open their mouths, they are generally very direct. Once they have decided to give their opinion, Finnish frankness matches the German; unpleasant or controversial issues are not sidestepped. This sudden directness is off-putting to those nationals who prefer delicacy or elegance of expression (Italian, French) or those who believe that one should bear only good news (Brazilians, Indonesians). Even the British, though appreciative of Finnish frankness, occasionally find them a bit brusque. This is perhaps the only area where Finns upset the Japanese (with whom they normally get along famously), for in Japan direct statements, especially if tinged with criticism, are completely taboo. Americans, on the other hand, like Finnish frankness.

Realism

Finns, partly as a result of their hard, somewhat unlucky history, are realists and pragmatists of the first degree. They rarely enthuse or indulge in pleasant speculation. Foreigners new to Finland talk of Finnish pessimism. Many, but not all, Finns see themselves as pessimistic or melancholy; climate plays a part in this perception. In my view Finns are not pessimists; rather, they have a built-in reluctance to promise more than they are sure they can deliver.

Forecasts of profit and progress will always be muted. The managing director of a solid company that had just had a very good year financially refused to be drawn into optimistic estimates of the following year's prospects. "It can only go down from here," he said, with a face the length of a violin. A by-product of Finnish realism is accuracy, whether dealing in facts and figures or assessing a changing situation.

Common Sense

When things go awry or on the occasion when Finns are dazzled by foreigners' charisma, they fall back on common sense. It is a characteristic shared by the four Scandinavian countries and serves as a guideline for Nordic regional cooperation at various levels right up to the smoothly functioning Nordic Council. In the EU committees, Finnish common sense is an admirable antidote to Latin rhetoric and altiloquence and is appreciated by the British, Dutch, and other Nordics.

The Finnish Cultural Black Hole

A cultural black hole (CBH), in my loose definition, is "an undiscussable core belief of such intense gravity that it transcends or distorts any other beliefs, values, or set of principles that enter inside the spherical boundary of its gravitational field. It absorbs, indeed swallows up, the precepts held by the 'victim.'"

To carry the imagery further, just as in the case of the cosmic black hole, where light can enter but never escape, we might see a parallel where such enlightenment as might be offered by a different set of cultural values belonging to the "approaching body" loses all impact as it falls into the CBH and disappears into blackness, nothingness, obliteration.

Do such things ever happen? Yes, they do, all the time. Cosmic black holes, as scientists admit, are still in the hypothetical stage; none has yet been positively identified. CBHs, on the contrary, permeate the surface of the globe. Classical CBHs often have political or religious origins. Unbridled patriotism and religious fanaticism are cases in point.

"My country, right or wrong" is a CBH, though it sounds good in times of war. This particular CBH, sucking in the normal rational and humanistic beliefs of a British soldier, enables him to shoot a German or Argentinian soldier with whom he shares a host of Western and universal values and morals, and a cultural heritage. The trenches of the First World War were both physical and cultural black holes, accounting for a massive distortion of views and (unfortunately) destruction of millions of lives of otherwise peaceful British, German, and French young men.

"There is only one God, Allah, and Muhammad is his prophet" is a CBH, inasmuch as the assertion, when absolute, brooks no argument, dissent, or alternative. A Muslim, though perfectly amenable to reason and open to debate, influence, or persuasion in other areas, may be completely intransigent and intractable if your argument impinges on the credibility of Islam.

Most of us own a cultural black hole or two, and we frequently drag in others who approach us if they dare to challenge our particular CBH. They may be sucked in as we devalue their discourse and subordinate it to our indisputable credo. Often we are unaware that we are doing this.

Take, for instance, the American Dream, which underpins the mentality of the mainstream American culture (not the subcultures).

Americans imbued with this spirit or credo firmly believe that the Dream exists and is obtainable only on American soil; no other dream can coexist with it.

Other CBHs are more benign, though no less powerful in their effect on their environment. In Japan, the concept of "face" is a CBH. Few nationalities easily accept losing face, though some handle it much better than others. If in countries such as France and the U.S. overconfidence and being overtly opinioned are CBH-related, in Finland the opposite is the case.

The Finn has an obsessive talent for self-effacement and ultra-taciturnity, where opinions are strongly held but often unvoiced. The manager of a Finnish engineering company told me recently that he had sent fifteen of his engineers for three weeks to service machines in a South American country. After the engineers returned, the South American managers refused to pay the bill, saying that they had never seen the engineers and did not believe they had really been there! Modesty and self-deprecation are not unattractive values, so a CBH is not necessarily always entirely negative, though it complicates communication in no small measure!

Finns are an adaptable, tolerant, and generally easygoing culture. Politeness is natural to their calm character. However, uneasiness with fast-talking foreigners can lead to distrust and often causes Finns to seem abrupt in their conversation. This abruptness is also linked to their own lack of talkativeness or grand speeches when Finns talk amongst themselves. They are often worried about the accuracy of their English language usage and tend to opt for saying less rather than risk the possibility of making errors. Silence is problematic for many cultures, but you should expect, understand, and show respect for it in your dealings with Finns.

THE FINNISH COMMUNICATOR

Much has been written about Finnish weaknesses in international communication situations, and it is no myth. Finns often appear as reluctant communicators and frequently fail to make the required impact when they speak. However, Finns have hidden strengths in this area, and more often than not, they aren't aware of them.

The Finns' strengths lie in their values and code of behavior, not in their expressiveness. The dilemma of the Finns is that they have Western European values cloaked in an Asian communication style; the two are in a sense incompatible. European values are determinate, logical, often Hegelian. In Northern Europe, especially, they tend to be "black and white." Asian values are less cut and dried, more ambiguous and peripheral. The Asian communication pattern—hesitant, deferential, ambivalent, always restrained—is an admirable medium for Asian values. In Finland it is a bad match.

Sandwiched between Swedish and Russian bosses in a cold climate, Finns had no incentive to open their mouth unless they were asked to. Not only was it more prudent to remain quiet, but it also suited their view of society. "Those who know do not speak; those who speak do not know" is a second-century Chinese proverb that the Finns, like the Japanese, do not quarrel with. In Finland, silence

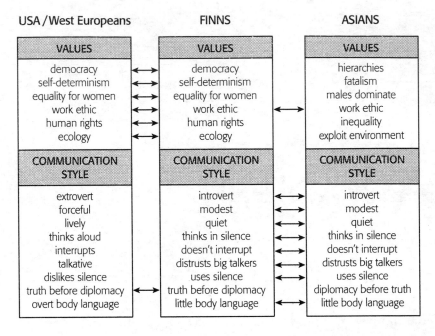

FIGURE 7.1   Finnish Values/Communication Dilemma

is not equated with failure to communicate; it is an integral part of social interaction. In Finland it is considered impolite or inappropriate to force one's opinions on others—it is more appropriate to nod in agreement, smile quietly, and avoid opinionated argument or discord.

In the Anglo-Saxon world and in Latin and Middle Eastern countries, talking has another function. In England the well-known habit of discussing the weather with neighbors or even strangers shows not only the preoccupation of the English with their fickle climate but also their desire to show solidarity with and friendliness toward their interlocutor (see Figure 7.1). This sociable discourse is even more evident in the U.S., Canada, and Australia, where speech is a vital tool for getting to know people and establishing a quick relationship. In France fluency of speech is regarded as an important

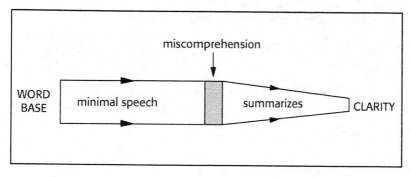

FIGURE 7.2   Finnish Communication Pattern

social attribute. The French may seem to have verbal diarrhea to the Finn, but they see themselves as intelligent, coherent, well trained, and communicative. The American habit of "thinking aloud" is a communicative gambit designed to gain the confidence of the listener, to share ideas that can then be discussed and modified. The Finn listens with a kind of horror, for in Finland a statement is a sort of commitment to stand by, not to change, twist, or contradict in the very next breath.

Finns are among the world's best listeners and are trained not to interrupt but to respect and value each other's remarks and to give careful consideration to the opinions and proposals of others. Concentration levels are high. They may give little or no feedback to a business presentation. Among themselves, they often feel very little pressure to contribute actively to discussion. Active listening (showing interest and involvement in the conversation) is rare, so when other nationalities meet Finns, they may feel quite uncomfortable with the Finns' lack of interruptions or comments.

The Finnish skill in listening and their reluctance to communicate swiftly stem from the "reactive" element in the Finnish mindset. Before we can discuss the Finnish reactive communication style (and the two opposing styles—multi-active and linear-active), we must have an understanding of these styles (see Figure 7.2).

Cultural Categories of Communication

Although there have been many models of cultural categorization with respect to communication types, my own research and experience has led me to believe in a three-category classification of cultures that relates directly to communication styles. I present these briefly below.

Linear-Active Cultures

Linear-active people tend to be task-oriented, highly organized planners who complete action chains by doing one thing at a time, preferably in accordance with a linear agenda. They prefer straightforward and direct discussion, sticking to facts and figures that they have obtained from reliable sources. Speech is for information exchange, and they talk and listen in equal proportions. They are truthful rather than diplomatic and do not fear confrontation, adhering to logic rather than emotions. Linear-active people are process-oriented and brief on the telephone; they respond quickly to written communication.

Multi-Active Cultures

Multi-active people are loquacious and impulsive, and they attach great importance to feelings and relationships; they are very people-oriented. They like to do many things at the same time and are poor followers of agendas. Their conversation is roundabout and animated, and they try to speak and listen at the same time. Interruptions are frequent, and pauses in conversation are few. Multi-active people are uncomfortable with silence and seldom experience or permit it. Written communication has less effect than oral, and they prefer to get their information directly from people.

Reactive Cultures

Reactive cultures are called "listening cultures." People from reactive cultures rarely initiate action or discussion, preferring first to listen and to establish the other's position, then react to it and formulate their own reaction. Reactives listen before they leap. They are the world's best listeners inasmuch as they concentrate on what the speaker is saying, do not let their minds wander, and rarely, if ever, interrupt a speaker during a conversation or presentation. Reactives don't always respond immediately after a speech or presentation is finished. A decent period of silence after the speaker has stopped shows respect for the weight of the remarks, which must be considered unhurriedly and with due deference.

Even when a reactive-culture representative begins his reply, he is unlikely to voice any strong opinion forthwith. A more probable tactic is to ask further questions on what has been said in order to clarify the speaker's intent and aspirations. Japanese, particularly, go over each point many times in detail to make sure there are no misunderstandings. Chinese take their time to assemble a variety of strategies that would avoid discord with the initial proposal.

The Reactive Mindset

Reactive cultures are to be found in Japan, China, Taiwan, Singapore, Korea, Turkey, and Finland. Several other East Asian countries, though occasionally multi-active and excitable, have certain reactive characteristics. In Europe, only the Finns are strongly reactive, but Swedes and other Nordic cultures also share some reactive traits.

Reactive peoples are introverts; they distrust a surfeit of words and consequently are adept at subtle nonverbal communication. Americans and other linear-active people find reactive tactics hard to fathom, since they do not slot into the linear system (question/reply, cause/effect). Multi-active people, accustomed to extrovert behavior, find Finns inscrutable—giving little or no feedback.

In reactive cultures the preferred mode of communication is monologue—pause—reflection—monologue. If possible, one lets the other side deliver his or her monologue first. It is rather like asking

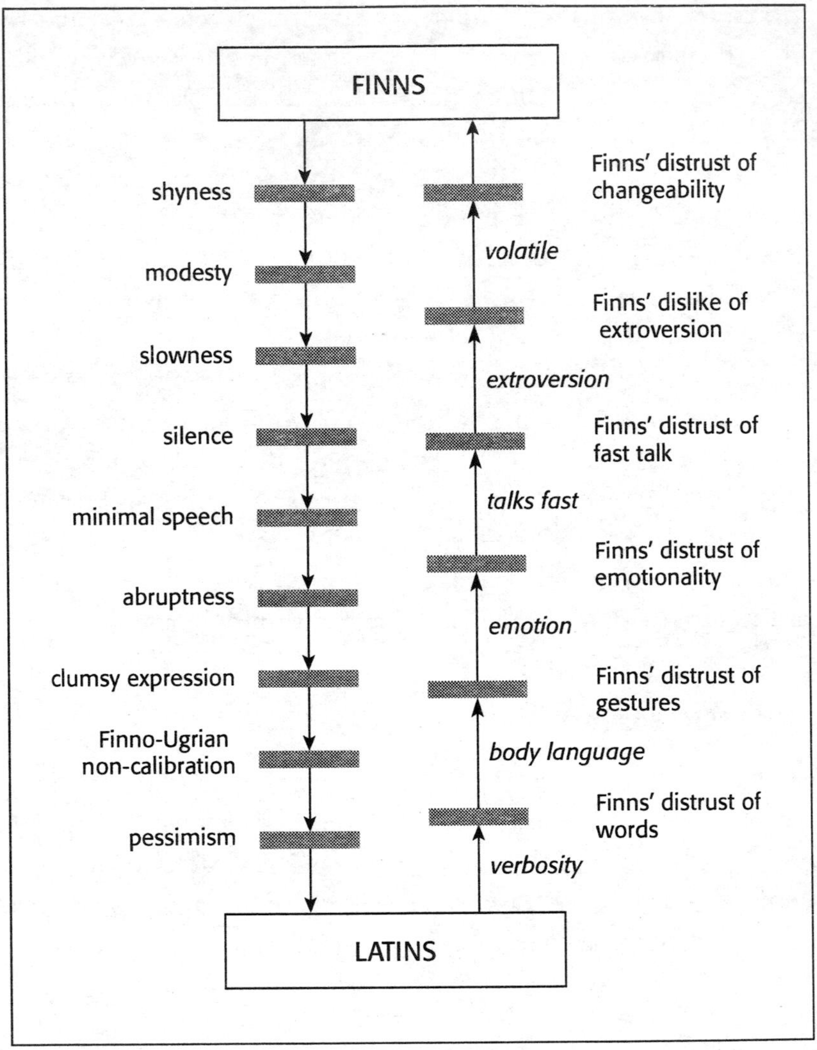

FIGURE 7.3   Barriers to Communication

the other side to bat first at cricket or baseball. In linear-active or multi-active cultures, the communication mode is a *dialogue*. One interrupts the other's "monologue" by frequent comments, even questions, which signify polite interest in what is being said. As soon as the other person stops speaking, one takes up one's turn immediately, since the Westerner, particularly an American, has an extremely weak tolerance of silences.

People belonging to reactive cultures not only tolerate silences well but regard them as a very meaningful, almost refined, part of discourse, as mentioned above. The opinions of the other party are not to be taken lightly or dismissed with a snappy or flippant retort. Clever, well-formulated arguments require—deserve—lengthy silent consideration.

Finns display Asiatic rather than European communication patterns. Being reactive by nature, Finns encourage others to speak first and respond carefully and usually after a pause. Finns value silence and will often use this when communicating as a sign of respect, without negative meaning. Statements are regarded as promises and are therefore delayed until the speaker is sure of his/her intentions. Finnish communication is typically frank and direct; exaggerated or emotive content and rhetoric are not welcomed or are seen as inappropriate and even humorous.

The American, having delivered his sales pitch in Helsinki, leans forward and says, "Well, Pekka, what do you think?" If you ask a Finn what he *thinks,* he begins to think. Finns, like Asians, think in silence. Another American, asked the same question, might well jump to his feet and exclaim, "I'll tell you what I think!" allowing no pause to punctuate the proceedings or interfere with Western "momentum." Finnish and Asian momentum takes much longer to achieve. One can compare reactions to handling the gears of a car. Multi-active persons go immediately into first gear, which enables them to put their foot down to accelerate (the discussion), then they pass quickly through second and third gears as the argument intensifies. Reactive cultures prefer to avoid "crashing through" the gearbox. Too many revs might cause damage to the engine (intercourse). The big wheel turns more slowly at first and the foot is put down gently. But when momentum is finally achieved, it is likely to be maintained and, what is more, tends to be in the right direction.

The reactive monologue mode of communication will accordingly be context-centered and will presume a considerable amount of knowledge on the part of the listener. Because the listener is presumed knowledgeable, the Finn will often be satisfied with expressing his thought with *half-utterances,* indicating that the listener can fill in the rest. It is a kind of compliment one pays one's interlocutor. At such times multi-active people are more receptive than linear-oriented people, who thrive on clearly expressed linear argument.

Finns not only rely on utterances and abbreviated statements to further the conversation, they also indulge in other Asian habits that can cause confusion. They are, for instance, "roundabout," using impersonal verbs ("one is leaving") or the passive voice ("one of the machines seems to have been tampered with") either to deflect blame or with the general aim of politeness.

As Finns tend to use names in their conversations less frequently than Americans or other Europeans do, the impersonal, vague nature of the discussion is further accentuated. The Finnish comparative lack of eye contact, as I've discussed, does not help the situation. Finns or Japanese, embarrassed by each other's stare, seek eye contact only at the beginning of the discussion or when they wish their opponents to take their "turn" in the conversation. Asian inscrutability (often appearing on a Finn's face as a sullen expression) adds to the feeling that the discussion is leading nowhere.

Small talk does not come easily to those from reactive cultures. Finns tend to regard questions such as "Well, how goes it?" as direct questions and may take the opportunity to voice a complaint. On other occasions their over-long pauses or slow reactions cause Americans or Latins to think Finns are slow-witted or have nothing to say. A high-ranking delegation from the Bank of Finland told me recently that they found it hard to get a word in at international meetings. How can we make an impact? they asked. The Japanese suffer even more in this type of gathering.

One should always bear in mind that the actual content of the response delivered by a person from a reactive culture represents only a small part of the significance surrounding the event. Context-centered utterances inevitably attach more importance not to *what* is said, but *how* it is said, *who* said it, and what is *behind* what is said. Also, what is *not* said may be the main point of the reply.

Self-disparagement is another favorite tactic of reactive cultures such as Finland, as I discussed in Chapter 6. It eliminates the possibility of offending someone's self-esteem; it may draw the opponent into praising one's conduct or decisions. One must beware, however, of presuming that self-disparagement is connected with a weak position.

Reactive cultures excel in subtle, subvocal utterances that compensate for the absence of frequent interjections. Finns, Japanese, and Chinese alike are noted for their sighs, almost inaudible groans, and agreeable grunts. A sudden intake of breath in Finland indicates agreement, not shock, as it would in the case of a Latin.

Finally, reactive peoples have large reserves of energy. They are economical in movement and effort and do not waste time reinventing the wheel. Though they always give the impression of having power in reserve, they are seldom aggressive.

The Data-Oriented Finn

Interaction between different peoples involves not only methods of communicating but also the process of gathering information. This brings us to the question of "dialogue-oriented" cultures and "data-oriented" cultures. In a data-oriented culture people do research to produce lots of information, which is then acted upon. Swedes, Germans, Finns, Americans, the Swiss, and Northern Europeans in general love to gather solid information and move steadily forward from this database. The communications and information revolution is a dream come true for those from data-oriented cultures. It provides them quickly and efficiently with what dialogue-oriented cultures already know.

People from dialogue-oriented cultures see events and business possibilities "in context" because they already possess an enormous amount of information through their own personal information network. Which are the dialogue-oriented cultures? Examples are the Italians and other Latins, Arabs, and Indians. People from one of these cultures will be well informed about the facts surrounding a deal since they will already have queried, discussed, and gossiped within their circle of friends, business acquaintances, and extensive family connections. The Japanese (basically listeners) may be even better informed, since the very nature of Japan's web society involves them in incredibly intricate information networks operational during schooldays, college, university, Judo and Karate clubs, student societies; developed intelligence systems; and family and political connections.

Dialogue-oriented, multi-active people are knee-deep in information. The Finn's lack of gregariousness again proves a hindrance. By upbringing, as a data-oriented, reactive type, Finns are taught *not to pry*—inquisitiveness gains no points in society; gossip is even worse. What their database cannot tell them they try to find out through official channels—embassies, chambers of commerce, circulated information sheets, perhaps hints provided by friendly companies with experience in the country in question. In business, especially when negotiating, information is power. Sweden, Norway, Australia, New Zealand, and several other data-oriented cultures, as well as Finns, will have to expand and intensify their intelligence-gathering networks in the future if they are to compete with information-rich France, Japan, Italy, Korea, Taiwan, and Singapore. It may well be that the EU itself will develop into a hothouse exchange of business information to compete with the Japanese network.

Nonverbal Communication Patterns

In the field of human communication, body language is extremely important, and psychologists tell us that our verbal message represents only 20 percent or less (some say far less) of what we actually convey to our interlocutor. The other 80 percent is transmitted by body language—that is to say, gestures, facial expressions, and other physiological manifestations.

Finns and Japanese, unlike Americans or Latins, do not seem to have any body language—an assumption that causes cultural shock for first-time visitors in Finland and Japan. I say do not seem, because in fact Finns and Japanese do use body language that is well understood by fellow nationals in each country.

Finns and Japanese have to be good "body watchers," as the verbal messages in their countries are kept at a minimum. In the Finnish and Japanese cultures, upbringing and training discourage gesticulations, exaggerated facial expressions, and uninhibited manifestations of glee, sorrow, love, hate, hope, disappointment, or triumph. In both societies the control and disciplined management of such emotions leads to the creation of a much more restrained type of body language, which is so subtle that it goes unnoticed by the American eye. Finns and Japanese are able to detect nonverbal messages in each other's culture, as their own nationals behave in a similar manner. As Finns and Japanese are accustomed to looking for minimal signs, the blatantly demonstrative body language of Italians, Arabs, and sometimes Americans produces strong culture shock for them. It is as if someone used to listening to the subtle melodies of Chopin or Mozart were suddenly thrown into a modern club. The type of message, the color, the visual impact, and, above all, the decibel level—all shock and irritate Pekka and Ichiro.

The danger is, of course, that overreaction sets in—a judgmental reaction that causes the Japanese and Finns alike to consider Americans and Germans as charging bulls, the French as too "clever," Italians as overly emotional, and even Danes as a bit slick.

In the case of Finns, differences of behavior that they see among the linear-active cultures are quickly reconciled. The internationalizing Finnish male is generous in making allowances for the smooth-talking Dane or Englishman, the boisterous German, the condescending Swede, and the always-in-a-hurry, money-minded American. It is, on the other hand, confrontation with the distinctly multi-active peoples that causes him persistent mental discomfort. Apart from that, he has to find his way forward toward communication and empathy with these people, with whom he may be in an ongoing trading relationship or even joint venture or acquisition. Similarly, linear-active and multi-active peoples need to practice the art of reading subtle Finnish nonverbal language.

Eyes

If we start with the eyes—among the more expressive parts of the body—we find that most cultures make more use of them in conversation than do the Finns. A Finnish male likes initial eye contact while introducing himself and shaking hands in the American manner, but he avoids significant use of it after that. Normally he looks at his interlocutor with sufficient attention when the other speaks but looks away when he gives his own reply. This is sometimes called "subordinate" eye behavior. As neither speaker is subordinate, reciprocal pretense that oneself is subordinate indicates a non-hostile approach appropriate to discussion between two egalitarian Finns. In multi-active cultures, where power distance between people is greater, the speaker will maintain close eye contact all the time he delivers his or her message. This is particularly noticeable in Spain, Greece, and Arab countries. In these countries, it is easy to detect what the "pecking order" is by observing the eye behavior of the people involved. Lower-ranking people tend to look at superiors, who ignore them unless they are in direct conversation with them. When anyone cracks a joke or says something controversial, all the subordinates' eyes will switch immediately to the chief personage to assess his (or her) reaction.

Close eye contact (Finns and Japanese would call it "staring") implies dominance and reinforces one's position and message. In Japan this is considered improper and rude. Japanese avoid eye contact 90 percent of the time, looking at a speaker's neck while the speaker talks and at their own feet or knees when they speak themselves. Americans, on the other hand, like medium to strong eye contact.

Mouth and Head

It is said that the mouth is one of the busiest parts of the human body, except in Finland, where men hardly use it (except for eating and drinking). This is, of course, not strictly true, but most societies not only use the mouth more for talking than the Finns but also convey a variety of expressive moods by the way they cast their lips. Charles De Gaulle, Fernandel, Saddam Hussein, Winston Churchill, Marilyn Monroe, and James Stewart made the mouth work overtime to reinforce their message or appeal. The tight-lipped Finn shrinks away from such communicative indulgences as the mouth shrug (French); the pout (Italian); the broad, trust-inviting smile of the American businessman; or even the fixed polite smile of the Asian.

Latins and other demonstrative peoples (including American subcultures) use about twenty-five different head gestures (toss, twist, side-jerk, tilt, etc.), which are too numerous to describe in detail in this work. Suffice it to say that Finns hardly use more than two (affirmative nod and negative shake), both of which are common to nearly all mankind, originating from age-old behavior. (The nod, approximating a bow, indicates submission to the will of the other.)

Shoulders, Arms, and Hands

Whereas Finns normally keep their shoulders still, multi-active peoples have very mobile shoulders. The Gallic shoulder shrug is well known from our observations of Fernandel, Maurice Chevalier, Jean Gabin, and Yves Montand and is not unknown in Hollywood. Latins keep their shoulders back and down when tranquil and observant, and push them up and forward when alarmed, anxious, or hostile.

Arms are used little by Finns during conversation. In Italy, Spain, and South America they are an indispensable element in one's communicative weaponry. Frequent gesticulating with the arms is one of the features that Finns find hardest to tolerate or imitate. It is inherently associated in the Finnish mind with insincerity, overdramatization, emotionality, and therefore unreliability. As far as touching is concerned, however, the arm is the most neutral of body zones, and even Finns will take guests by the elbow to guide them through doorways or indulge in the occasional arm pat to deserving subordinates or approaching friends.

The hands are among the most expressive parts of the body. Kant called them "the visible parts of the brain." Italians watching Finnish hands may be forgiven for thinking that Finns have sluggish brains, though practiced Finn-watchers know better. Northern peoples undeniably use their hands less expressively than Latins or Arabs, who recognize them as a brilliant piece of biological engineering. There are so many signals given by the use of the hands that we cannot consider them all here. Finns tend to shun obscene gestures with fingers, only too common in Latin cultures and in North America.

Legs, Feet, and Gait

As we move even further down the body, less evident but equally significant factors come into play. Finns participate in "leg language" like Americans and everybody else. As no speech is required, leg language inflicts no strain on them. In general the legs-together when in a seated position basically signifies defensiveness, against a background of formality, politeness, or subordination. Most people keep their legs together when applying for a job. It indicates correctness of attitude. This position is quite common in Finland at first meetings but changes to "legs crossed" as discussions become more informal. Formal negotiators such as Germans or Japanese can go through several meetings maintaining the legs-together position.

There are at least half a dozen different ways of crossing your legs, the most formal being crossing ankles only, the average being crossing the knees, and the most relaxed and informal being the ankle-on-knee cross so common in North America. Finns generally progress as far as knee-over-knee, though the ankle-knee cross is frequently seen when they are talking to other Finns.

It is said that the feet are the most honest part of the body. Although we are self-conscious about our speech or eye and hand movements, we actually forget what our feet are doing most of the time. The honest Finns, therefore, send out as many signals with their feet as the Latins do. Foot messages include tapping on the floor (boredom), flapping up and down (want to escape), heel lifting (desperate to escape), or multi-kicking from a knees-crossed position (desire to kick the other speaker). Finnish reticence sometimes reduces the kicking action to wiggling the toes up and down inside one's shoes, but the desire is the same. Overt foot stamping in anger, common in Italy and other Latin countries, is not used in Finland or the United States.

There are more than thirty different types of gait, or ways of walking, which we cannot cover here. Suffice it to say that Finns walk in a fairly neutral manner, avoiding the Latin bounce, the American swagger, and the German march. It is more of a brisk plod, especially brisk in winter, when the Spanish dawdle would lead to possible frostbite.

Communication Patterns in the Workplace

The Finnish communication style isolates Finland in international discourse. One hears the same messages whispered over and over again: "Foreigners talk so fast—we are slow by comparison—we can't learn languages—our pronunciation is terrible—it's because our own language is so difficult—foreigners are more experienced than we are—they are cleverer and often deceive us—they don't mean what they say—we can't rely on them—we are the truest people."

At meetings, Finns believe in saying only that which is absolutely necessary. Like the Japanese, they do not really trust words. If their original proposal is considered unclear, they repeat it in summarized form, assuming that is the best route to clarity. ("What I really meant was A, B, and C.")

Having lived many years in Finland, I have great respect for and sympathy with the admirable reserve and obvious sincerity of the Finnish people. But the fact is that Pekka Virtanen will have to enter the verbal fray, for the truth is Europe can manage without Finnish industry, but the converse is not the case. The "nichemanship" strategy of Finnish companies has proved itself a valuable option for a country severely limited by the smallness of its home market. But at the same time, Finnish industry cannot afford to neglect any viable overseas markets and there is an urgent requirement to get on trading terms with Europeans, Americans, Arabs, Japanese, and other Eastern nations. Japan, with its similar communicative style, has already set up factories and offices throughout the world and is currently grappling with the cultural and communicative problems of working side-by-side with foreign nationals or actually managing them. Finland, admittedly on a smaller scale, is in the process of doing the same.

Finnish firms and managers have begun to raise their awareness of intercultural problems, throw off some of their complexes, and consider carefully their approach to various nationalities. Finns *can* speak languages (better than most people), they *can* organize, and they possess the virtues of punctuality, well-ordered activity, work ethic, calm planning, and so on that they inherited from their environment and history. They must understand that other peoples *very* different from them, seemingly disorganized, emotional, even chaotic, certainly have their own virtues and may often be right. Finns will do well if they maintain their own personality and values and combine these with others' manners and customs in an attempt to find formulas for smooth management in a cross-cultural situation.

Finns are not the only ones who need to compromise; others also need to adapt. In conversation with Finns, one should listen very carefully to what they say, as they tend not to repeat themselves unless requested to do so. Moreover, there is a strong correlation in Finland between thought, word, and deed, which means that Finns are in all probability telling you what they really intend to do. This kind of "guarantee" does not exist in dealings with Latins or Arabs, who have a much more emotive attitude toward words.

Statements made by Finns are the end product of meticulous, unhurried thinking, where pros and cons and *your* position have been carefully considered. They are telling you what they are willing to do and how far they will go. They do not expect you to try to change their position.

Americans or Italians when discussing proposals will use impressive, persuasive powers and expect a lot of give and take as the discussion progresses. Words, words, and more words will be brought to bear on the issue. This is not the way to deal with Finns, as they have taken up a position and will not cede it easily. The more subjective and voluble you become, the more obstinate and tight-lipped they will appear.

A better approach is to acknowledge the strength of the Finns' argument and study it for a while in silence. Finns do not expect you to respond immediately or spontaneously. After some time you may compare the two positions, commenting gently on the areas of difference and asking how both sides could modify their stance to narrow the divergence. What do *you* think, Pekka? Pekka and colleagues will have another good think, and the odds are that they will cooperate. Finns accept changes if you do not try to foist them upon them.

Americans and Britons, with the advantage of the language (it is unlikely that you will be negotiating in Finnish), should be economical with words, though not with the truth. Finns are paying you and your culture an enormous compliment by wielding your language with consummate skill and even fondness. Anglo-Saxons should repay this compliment by speaking in a clear, nonidiomatic manner, devoid of slang, jargon, or *double entendre*. Some imitation of the Finnish communication style is advisable, for instance, adherence to facts, a logical progression, and frequent summaries of the issues. Britons should resist their temptation to wax eloquent and hold the floor. Americans should remember that a fixed, broad smile may be counterproductive with introvert Finns.

Women as Communicators

Finnish women require a separate section because they are more communicative than Finnish males (for more on Finnish women, see Chapter 12). When interacting with women, you must bear the following in mind:

1. The equality of the sexes in Finland is a functioning reality.
2. The educational level of Finnish women rivals or exceeds that of any other nationality.
3. Finnish women are communicative, exploratory, and directly engaging.
4. Some emotionality on the part of Finnish women may mean heightened sensitivity to messages and the ability to read them. This could result in a more holistic, all-embracing (conceptual) approach to many issues.
5. Some nationalities, for example, Italian or Portuguese, sometimes find it easier to approach a (Nordic) woman than a man.

There is no doubt that Finnish women will play an important role in the EU connection.

LEADERSHIP

*"Given the increased globalisation of industrial
organisations and increased interdependencies among
nations, the need for better understanding of cultural
influences on leadership and organisational practices
has never been greater."*

— "Cultural Influences on Leadership and Organisations:
Project Globe," WHARTON SCHOOL OF MANAGEMENT,
UNIVERSITY OF PENNSYLVANIA

Different cultures have diverse concepts of leadership. Leaders can be born, elected, or trained and groomed. Others seize power or have leadership thrust upon them. Leadership can be autocratic or democratic, collective or individual, meritocratic or unearned.

It is not surprising that business leaders (managers) often wield their power in conformity with the national set-up; for instance, a confirmed democracy like Sweden produces low-key democratic managers; Arab managers are good Muslims; Chinese managers usually have government or party affiliations.

Leaders cannot readily be transferred from culture to culture. Japanese prime ministers would be largely ineffective in the United States; American politicians would fare badly in most Arab countries; mullahs would not be tolerated in Norway. By the same token, it is hardly surprising that business leaders find the transition from one culture to another fraught with difficulties. Such transfers, however, are becoming more and more common with the globalization of business; therefore, the composition of international teams, particularly the choice of their leaders, requires careful thought. Autocratic French managers need to tread warily in consensus-minded Japan or Sweden. Courteous Asian leaders will have to adopt a more vigorous style in argumentative Holland or theatrical Spain if they wish to hold the stage. German managers sent to Australia should prepare themselves for the irreverence of their staff and their apparent lack of respect for authority.

The Future Is Finnish

The dominant U.S. model of leadership—the "great man" or "business hero"—has foundered. General Electric's charismatic Jack Welch has fallen from grace, together with senior executives from WorldCom, Enron, and Arthur Andersen, among others. Japan, with its hesitancy to confront uncomfortable truths, and the collapse of its banks, no longer serves as an alternative model for organizational practices. While corporate America in particular, and the world in general, seems to be losing faith not only in its leaders, but even in its very idea of leadership,* perhaps we can learn from a style that is founded—as Jorma Ollila himself recently suggested in a speech to Finnish war veterans—on ethical norms and values that are peculiar to this remote but intriguing nation.

Finland's Rising Star

At cross-century Finland could claim to be the most advanced country in Europe. Jointly with Singapore and the United States, Finland is foremost in global competitiveness and, along with Norway, is in

---

* A survey by Kofi Annan in 2000 showed that two-thirds of the world's citizens—including the advanced democracies such as the U.S.—did not feel themselves represented by their governments, with the only exception being the Nordic democracies.

first place for sustainability of development. Voted in a recent survey as the least corrupt country in the world, she is also world leader in literacy, mathematics, and science. Despite her small population, Finland is second in percentage of GDP spent on R&D and fourth in the filing of successful patents. Nokia, the country's economic star, was for some time Europe's biggest company by market capitalization and is generally regarded as Europe's fastest-moving enterprise, weathering storms while others have floundered. Finns have the highest per capita use of mobile phones and the greatest use of Internet. Finland was "the most technologically advanced in the world" according to the UN Development Report, 2001.

How has a small and remote country with no natural resources except timber managed to reorient itself so rapidly and profitably toward high-tech development and at the same time to weather the social changes and strains involved in the sputtering development of the EU and against a background of worldwide instability?

When we see this example of one of the world's most stable societies and best-managed economies, we have to assume that Finnish success is inevitably bound with the qualities of the Finns themselves. What kind of people are they?

Finnish Qualities

The *Economist* and the *Financial Times* wrote surveys at the end of the century entitled "The Future Is Finnish." In view of Finland's somewhat desperate situation in 1945, one of the questions on the survey was "What cultural changes have made these leaps forward possible?" An English "Finland watcher" who had observed the country's progress closely in the period 1952–2000 opined that little cultural change had in fact taken place. The basic ingredients for Finnish success came to the fore fifty years ago, for the most part undetected by a more boisterous international community. In an era of economic boom, spin doctors, and a general indulgence in hype and flamboyance, it was easy to miss the quiet advancement of an understated society like the Finnish. The Finn's "slow, reticent, apparently unresponsive behavior," so named by Swedes, Germans, and the French, among others, is actually a deceptive veneer covering a very modern individual. Finns have high standards of cleanliness, honesty, stamina, workmanship, reliability, safety, and education. They protect their environment and guard the health of their society. Ultimately, they inspire confidence and win friends. They offer their own friendship slowly and cautiously at first, but once given, it is of a lasting nature. They are keen on self-respect and inner harmony. They often work well in teams but frequently demonstrate individual lateral thinking and inventiveness. They like the idea of profit centers and accountability.

Such is the modern Finn, utilizing state-of-the-art technology and the facilities of the Information Revolution but clinging to the age-old rural values of common sense, straightforwardness, steadiness, reliability, simplicity, and hatred of bombast and debt—an image not very different from that projected by the Finnish generation of 1952.

Jorma Ollila, Nokia's dynamic CEO, included these same basic Finnish virtues when he was asked in 2002 about the reasons for his and his company's success. He answered that Nokia has gained its strength from its firm underpinning of uncomplicated, sincere, durable tenets taken straight from Finnish rural society.

Finnish Leadership

Finns, with their sense of (cultural) separateness, distrust of deviousness and verbosity, and their national obsession with achievement, can be led only by Finns. It is said that Stalin, when urged by advisers to occupy Finland, replied, "Leave them alone—they make difficult subjects." On all fronts, in war and peace, Finnish leadership has proven itself pragmatic, prudent, farsighted, and effective. The current stable and secure position of the Finnish state and the solidity of her social and commercial standing reflect both the efficacy and appropriateness of this leadership.

How can Finnish leadership be defined? If we first attempt a broad categorization, we can draw a comparison with some other cultural groups. These fall neatly into the tripartite cultural classification introduced in Chapter 7 (see also Figure 8.1).

- **Linear-actives**—the calm, factual, decisive planners (Germans, Swedes, Americans, Northern Europeans in general)
- **Multi-actives**—warm, emotional, loquacious, impulsive leaders (Arabs, Africans, South Americans, Southern Europeans)
- **Reactives**—courteous, outwardly amiable, accommodating, compromising, good listeners (Japanese, Chinese, and most Asians)

Finns, with their step-by-step planning and action orientation, fall clearly into the linear-active category but on closer scrutiny are

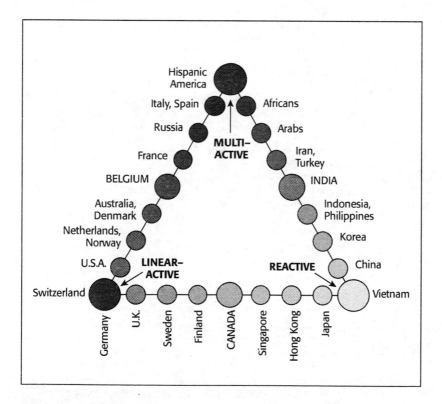

FIGURE 8.1   Cultural Types

observed to be somewhat hybrid in so far as they possess a goodly number of reactive tendencies. These are, among others, reticence, use of silence, humbleness, good listening without interruptions, long pauses between speech turns, concealment of feelings, and the belief that statements are promises. Respective positions on the linear-active, multi-active, and reactive axes are seen on the diagram on the previous page.

Management Style

The somewhat hybrid nature of Finnish behavior is also reflected in their management (leadership) style. If we look at managers' positions and stance vis-à-vis staff, we see striking differences even within Europe. French managers are among the most autocratic, as Figure 8.2 shows.

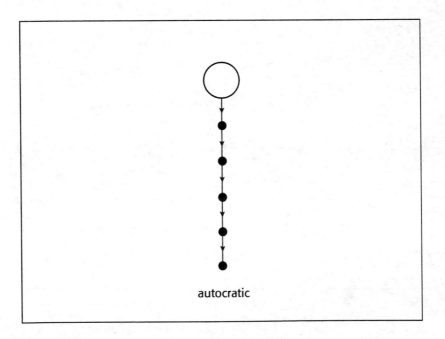

autocratic

FIGURE 8.2   French Leadership Style

In France, authority is centered around the chief executive. Top managers, who have usually been groomed in one of the *grandes écoles,* are well trained, charismatic, and extremely autocratic. They often appear to consult with middle managers, technical staff—even workers—but decisions are generally personal and orders are top-down. Managers at this elite level are rarely fired when they make blunders.

In contrast, the Swedish leadership style is the most democratic, as Figure 8.3 shows.

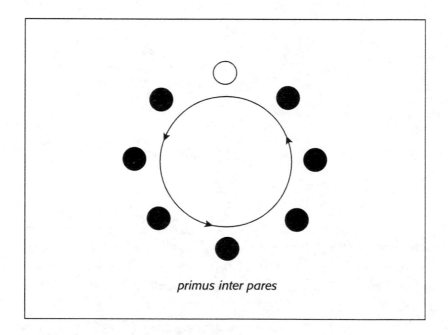

primus inter pares

FIGURE 8.3   Swedish Leadership Style

Swedish managers sit in the ring, consulting with all executive-level staff and often with quite subordinate staff members. It is said Swedish managers wield power by appearing not to be powerful. This style, ubiquitous in Sweden and popular with Swedes, is hardly conducive to rapid decision making.

If we compare the British CEO's style with the Swedish, we see that in many companies, he or she functions just outside the ring of managers but stays near enough for perhaps daily contact (and intervention). See Figure 8.4. Class differences may come into play.

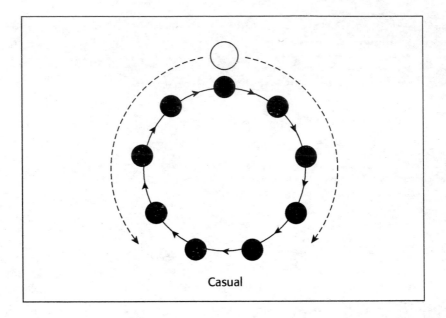

Casual

FIGURE 8.4   British Leadership Style

Finnish CEOs, when asked to compare their style with other Europeans, immediately rule out the French structure as premodern and outmoded. They tend to place themselves somewhere between the Swedes and the British—more democratic than the latter but more autocratic than the former.

Like many British, Finnish leaders exercise control from a position just outside and above the ring of upper-middle managers, who are allowed to make day-to-day decisions (see Figure 8.5). Finnish top executives have the reputation of being decisive at crunch time and do not hesitate to stand shoulder to shoulder with staff to help out during crises. Then they get out again.

If we look at Belbin's description of leader types on the next page, we see that at a strategic level the Finnish CEO qualifies as a team leader rather than as a solo leader. In Finland talent is sought out and speedily recognized, colleagues are developed and empowered, and funds are readily provided for research and development.

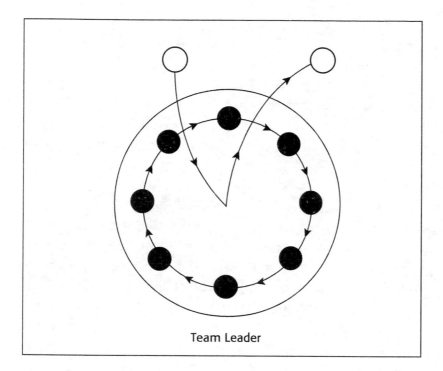

Team Leader

FIGURE 8.5   Finnish Leadership Style

Yet at the operational level, the image of the strong man (or woman) is not entirely absent from Finnish business. Managers of Finnish subsidiaries in Sweden often find themselves frustrated by the slow tempo and lack of decisiveness of Swedish managerial colleagues and have been known to come in hard for decisions and action.

TABLE 8.1   Leadership Types

Solo leader	Team leader
1. Plays unlimited role (interferes)	1. Chooses to limit role (delegates)
2. Strives for conformity	2. Builds on diversity
3. Collects acolytes	3. Seeks talent
4. Directs subordinates	4. Develops colleagues
5. Projects objectives	5. Creates mission

Also at the operational level the Finnish CEO confronts an issue common to managers of all nationalities—that of language and communication style. The relatively new subject of language of management explores the close connection between the style in which leaders address their own compatriots and the (national) language they use. Different languages are used in different ways and with a variety of effects. Understated British English contrasts sharply with exuberant, hyperbolic American, motivating in an entirely different manner.

Finnish—a language rich in vocabulary and manipulative particles, as we saw in Chapter 5—is an interesting vehicle for communication. Finnish managers are not averse to blowing hot and cold when they want things from their staff. They can be cold, terse, and factual in one mode, then switch to a richer, more flowery style when it suits their purpose. Finnish is more vibrant and sinewy than Scandinavian languages, with its inexhaustible, adjective-strewn vocabulary embellished by its fourteen case endings. These features give the speaker far more linguistic options than one can call on in most languages. Finns may not be fully aware of this facility, but it offsets nicely the national tendency toward reticence. Finnish managers, generally well educated, keep their richness of expression in reserve in general, day-to-day conversation, but occasionally they will "pull out all the stops" when praise, encouragement, or reprimand are appropriate.

At a recent management conference the CEO of one of Finland's top ten companies addressed key staff in the following manner. He

1. analyzed the challenges,
2. praised those present for achievements to date,
3. went into critical mode, being very frank and direct, without mentioning names,
4. became even more critical, highlighting serious errors made (very coldly critical at this stage),
5. "joined the ranks" to examine solutions,

6. removed himself from the ranks again to make strongly worded proposals,
7. attacked all extravagance ("Never waste a penny of company money"),
8. emphasized common sense as a way forward, and
9. ended on an optimistic, though pragmatic note. Straight face, no smiles.

The staff members, also straight-faced and unsmiling, seemed comfortable with the message and responded with an approving silence.

Traits of Finnish Leaders

The traits most commonly attributed to Finns, and by extension to Finnish leaders, are honesty, directness, reliability, pragmatism, rationality, decisiveness, result orientation, secularism, trust of perception, task orientation, respect for others, modesty, shyness, humility, introversion, use of silence, good listening, distrust of verbosity, concept of service, medium-term planning, combining individualism and teamwork, and alternating optimism and pessimism.

If we examine these characteristics according to the Lewis cultural framework (see Chapter 7 for complete explanation), they divide as shown in Table 8.2.

TABLE 8.2 Cultural Types

Linear-active	Multi-active	Reactive
Honesty	Medium-term planning	Respect for others
Directness		Modesty
Reliability	Combining individualism	Shyness
Pragmatism	and teamwork	Humility
Rationality		Introversion
Decisiveness		Use of silence
Result orientation	Alternating optimism and	Good listening
Secularism	pessimism	Distrust of verbosity
Trust of perception		Concept of service
Task orientation		

When Finnish managers are in linear-active mode, they differ very little in behavior from Germans, Swedes, Norwegians, Dutch, Britons, Canadians, and even Americans. The linear program is common to all. What differentiates the Finnish managerial style from that of the other Northern Europeans and Americans is the strong reactive element that permeates their comportment (see Chapter 7 and earlier in this chapter for more explanation of reactive style), a style unquestionably Asian rather than European. Shyness, modesty, humbleness, respect for others, introversion, good listening, and appropriate use of silence are highly visible traits in a wide arc of cultures all the way from Rangoon to Tokyo and throughout Southeast Asia.

Two reactive or Asian qualities, deep down in the Finnish psyche, that seem to influence their leadership style the most, are ones that any leader might benefit from. First, a respect for and harmony with nature and its forces—at a spiritual level—has a deep effect on both Finnish and Asian psyches, an influence that is favorable to business. A parallel from the East could be seen in the Chinese philosopher Lao Tzu, who emphasized flexibility as the wisest response to natural forces and change. Finns have been great adapters, to both seasonal and historical change. They appear to have an innate capacity to thrive and bounce back from adverse weather and historical and economic conditions because they are prepared, flexible, and agile.

These qualities serve admirably in the rapidly changing information society and when market conditions swing violently. Unfavorable economic gusts, such as war reparations to the former Soviet Union, and the recession at the beginning of the 1990s, are deftly turned into drivers for success. Nokia's reaction to the recent high-tech turndown, according to Lea Myyrylainen, manager of mobile interfaces and quoted in *Fortune* magazine, February 2002, was very Finnish: "We're going to show them. We are not afraid. We are going to push more." They like to calmly "guts it out."

Finns are accepting, even grimly humorous, in the face of the worst—including death, which is less of a taboo subject than in many cultures. These characteristics, existing in so many individuals as part of their basic psychology, make Finns collectively able to stand up to disaster in a measured way. They are equally calm in tragedy and triumph. And calm subjects immeasurably help a calm leader.

A second valuable Finnish quality is the favoring of action (the focused variety) above words. Väinö Linna's trilogy of novels, *Under the North Star,* starts "In the beginning was the swamp,* the hoe and Jussi." A job to do, the tool to do it with, and an individual who just gets on with it. What more needs to be said? The duty is clear without words.

Leadership through actions rather than words was exemplified in the twentieth century by Mahatma Gandhi, who influenced India and the rest of the world by what he did, more than by what he said. Gandhi's philosophical roots lay in the *Bhagavad Gita,* where spiritual bravery consists of right action rather than words. For Finns, closer to home for Westerners, this is not so much a philosophy as an irreducible part of their psyche, making them exceptionally good at implementation in business. The Protestant work ethic only served to confirm this trait.

Does the possession of a goodly number of Asian reactive traits help a Northern European put together an effective managerial style when doing business internationally? It would seem so. Japanese executives in Tokyo frequently comment on how acceptable Finnish managers are. Finns are among the fastest to gain trust from the Japanese and Chinese, largely on account of their quiet manner and the absence of "pushiness." In any environment, shyness and modesty free one from the arrogance that often springs from power. Finnish leaders are almost never arrogant, nor do they rely on charisma, often utilized by the French and other Latins. Rarely over-persuasive, Finns develop a capacity to cause others to follow them.

* The Finnish word for "swamp," *suo,* may well be the source for the name of the country, Suomi, and so be a metonym for Finland as a whole.

Balanced Leadership

Most successful Finnish companies subscribe to the principle of "balanced leadership," where a small group of senior executives complement each other with their varying skills. Nokia is the best-known example, where calm, perceptive Jorma Ollila gave free rein to the talents of his executive team: Ala-Pietilä, Kallasvuo, Alahuta, Vanjoki, Neuvo, and Sari Baldauf. Pekka Ketonen, and the management team at Vaisala, would be another example.

Finnish CEOs possess another quality that is by no means Asian and not completely European either: their capacity for openness and transparency—almost a religion at Nokia—and more common in the Nordic countries than anywhere else. Nordic companies tend to be flat; the CEO is normally fairly accessible, and nowhere is this more true than in Finland. Finnish companies have "delayered" better than most, and ideas permeate the organization through to the chief executive quickly. Autonomous groups are empowered and encouraged to find and manage their own resources. In open, flat organizations communication is two-way. In many other societies information being passed upward is normally slower than top-down directives, which causes hierarchies to persist in many societies.

Openness and a truly democratic spirit have led Finnish firms to support open, shared technologies. Both Nokia and Linux are good examples of this. They recognize that pure market forces, untempered by societal concerns, may lead to destructive decisions. For example, telecommunications standards that apply worldwide are good for everyone, as Nokia has pushed for. (In the battle of values across borders, it is revealing that a senior executive of Microsoft recently described Linux as "un-American.") Of course, once such standards are established, one can compete aggressively through more attractive products and an agile market-segmentation strategy that reflects and even fosters individual values and lifestyles.

In the End, Common Sense

Imbued with an innate modesty and self-imposed blindness to their virtues, Finns would be the last to paint themselves whiter than white. And of course there are notable exceptions to the rule. However, if actions, not good intentions, are how we should judge ethical standards, then Finns tend to live up to what they promise to a greater degree than many others.

In summary, Finnish leaders are successful because they have moved with the times, embraced and pursued technology, faced difficult periods with courage, combined Western energy with Eastern wisdom, and relied on their own resources rather than on help from others. The success of Finnish business reflects the success of the Finnish state. One outstanding quality has endured since independence, through two wars, and up to the present day. That is the Finnish capacity for common sense. Common sense is not, of course, the same throughout the world. In Sweden it is common sense to queue up to get on a bus. In Spain it is common sense to get on the bus first. In Finland it is common sense to appreciate that in the Information Age the world is so complex and uncertain that no single person can comprehend or deal with the whole. Instead, Finns concentrate on core business and intelligently manage the resources—human and material—that they have at their disposal.

CHAPTER
NINE

SUOMI-KUVA AND THE DIFFICULT FINN

The Finnish obsession with cultural relativism has an interesting by-product in the somewhat naïve, but enduring, *suomi-kuva* (Finland image). Wearing blue and white spectacles, the Finn sees others as stereotypes (the shifty Latin American, the stuffy Swede, etc.), but the Finn is also a practiced "autostereotyper" of the first degree. An autostereotype is the standardized mental picture held in common by members of a cultural group depicting an over-simplified image of themselves and their behavior. For some reason Finns in particular are eager, even anxious, to project this image to the outside world. Few foreigners abroad who inquire about Finland escape this benign brainwashing—and certainly none who arrive on its shores do.

The phenomenon of suomi-kuva is important because although it is only partly true and largely mythical, it determines the foreigner's attitude toward Finns both before and after getting to know them, and it subconsciously defines his or her role and style when interacting with Finnish nationals in social and business situations.

What Is a Finn?

Finnish university students, in a recent survey, answered the question, "What is a Finn?" with the following description:

> The typical Finn is quiet, silent, . . . shy, uncommunicative, reserved, introverted, a bit cold and stiff, distrustful, suspicious, hard to convince, stubborn, not very outgoing, and self-centered. He walls himself off, is not a very open personality, is a very "inside" person who is difficult to get in contact with, lacking in self-certainty, bad at English and foreign languages, and even if he knows English very well, he tries to avoid speaking it as much as possible.
>
> Out in the world he is inclined to listen to others rather than to speak himself, is pessimistic, always looks sad, doesn't laugh unless he is amused, doesn't have a very developed sense of humor, is not very helpful or friendly when you first meet him, is cold on the surface but friendly when you get to know him, and is not used to foreigners.
>
> He is rigid, conservative, old-fashioned, formal, polite but cold, serious-minded, precise, accurate, and interested in exact information. He wants things in black and white, means what he asks, and wants straight answers. He's got *sisu* (guts); at the same time he is very patriotic, hardworking, diligent, ambitious, reliable, honest (too honest sometimes), natural. He is one who wants to do things thoroughly, is sincere in action, and does what he has promised to do (no mañana mentality). He is one you can trust, a real friend once you get to know him, a true friend.
>
> The typical Finn goes to the sauna (which is not a sex place) at least once a week; it's an important place, and his home. He loves nature, sports, skiing, and privacy; he spends his spare time with his family; he can be a bit rude and impolite at times without knowing it, and he does not

have very good manners because he feels inferior if he is polite.

He has drinking problems: he loves his Koskenkorva vodka and drinks to get drunk, not during the week but during the weekends. He likes his beer, and he likes his Finnish sausage in the sauna. He likes to do business in the sauna, particularly "big business." He doesn't like to hear people say Finland is part of Russia; he loves his country, its nature, his language. He is proud to be a Finn; he is interested in hearing how you find him and if you like him, but he doesn't want to hear the truth. He has a hard time seeing and admitting his own faults. He likes himself, is sensitive, and he gets a heart attack because of all this.

One suspects that this composite description was somewhat tongue-in-cheek, as the students easily "rolled out" the popular stereotype, but the descriptions contain more than a kernel of truth. Finns can indeed be difficult or paradoxical, as we saw in Chapter 6; they can display a darker side.

For example, the Finns see themselves as essentially tolerant (which indeed they are in the main), but they have a tendency to secretly despise certain groups of people who fail to conform to some Finnish standards of comportment. These phobias include (1) verbosity, (2) displays of emotion, (3) extrovert body language, (4) persistent small talk, (5) lack of punctuality, and even (6) charisma. You may explain to a Finnish male that both reliable and unreliable Italians wave their arms when they speak, but often he will remain unconvinced. Latins have to work hard to convince Finns of their integrity. Americans put Finns off with their Hollywood smiles and voluble hype.

Another problem is that Finns, when annoyed, usually conceal their discontent and fail to speak up. They do not realize that an argumentative Frenchman would welcome interruptions from a Finn, whom he is desperately trying to open up. Both in social discourse and at international meetings, the Finns' failure to take their turn and speak out is only too common. Then when they do speak up (after a period of frustrated silence), they generally say too much—not in volume, but in vehemence. In other words, they don't "wrap things up" in nice words. Latins and even the British and Swedes expect more diplomacy or even coded speech and consequently may think Finns are socially clumsy. Japanese, who otherwise like Finns, find their directness outright rude.

Finns also seem to have a national tendency to suffer (alternately) from periodic inferiority and superiority complexes. They grimly criticize themselves, their company, other institutions, even their country for a while. Later they will be ultra-defensive, pointing out how Finns are superior (ultra-honest, never in debt, reliable, etc.) and impeccable in their morals, rectitude, and industrial (and artistic) products. They also are perfectionists, resolutely seeking perfection and high quality when often they cannot afford it. They hate to lose face, and besides, what would the neighbors say?

The Finns' desire to protect their face leads to another well-known trait of the difficult Finn—obstinacy. This has led many a well-meaning and flexible British or Swedish business colleague or partner to (despairingly) ask the question, "How do you get a Finn to change his mind?" The Finnish tendency to get into entrenched positions is part and parcel of the go-it-alone strategy, not far removed from the Cultural Lone Wolf phenomenon. If a Finn is not consulted early in the planning of an operation, he will develop his own concept of the project, it will solidify in a matter of days, and after that, he will not wish to budge from his position or opinion.

Finnish irritability, a by-product of their obsession with privacy, can be annoying to foreign visitors. This is observable in Finns' dislike of being too closely monitored when carrying out a task at work. Foreign managers look over Finnish shoulders at their peril. By the same token, Finnish shoppers abhor being followed or pestered by shop assistants. Finnish attendants know better than to intrude. A supervisor of a British clothes manufacturer—Next—

related that when she escorted a group of thirty foreign agents around a spring exhibition clockwise to present the new models, she was followed obediently by twenty-eight agents. Two agents, however, went around alone and unsupervised in a *counter-clockwise* direction. They were the Finn and the Estonian. When the supervisor asked them to join the group, they retorted, "We can make up our own mind."

On the subject of drinking, the Finns can offer few arguments in their defense. Statistics show that they are not only the biggest coffee drinkers in the world, but also the biggest consumers of alcohol. Spending around $450 per head per annum, they are well ahead of other Nordics (Swedes $303), Americans ($280), the French ($220), and even the Russians ($154).

It is true that Finnish tastes have swung away from hard liquor toward wine in recent years, but the fact remains that drunks are more visible on Finland's city streets (and in railway stations) than in any other major country, with the possible exception of Russia. Finnish social drinking, while moderately restrained in the middle classes, rarely follows the elegant wining rituals so often visible in Italy, France, Spain, and to some extent the United States and Britain. Many Finns admit that the purpose of drinking is to get drunk. They do not imbibe overmuch during the week, but weekend binges from Friday night to Sunday afternoon form a regular part of Finnish life, especially, but not only, among working classes.

The Finns have greatly improved their diet and many have stopped smoking, but it is remarkable how a nation with such fine records in health and environmental management has so far failed to rein in the national desire for alcohol.

Suomi-Kuva through the Years

Suomi-kuva, with its endearing, gutsy, annoying, comical, and darker sides, has endured through the years, and it shows no signs of an early demise.

Suomi-Kuva 1937

The first suomi-kuva I got was projected to me not by the Finnish Tourist Information Service but by prewar books in school libraries. As early as 1937 one could read English books on athletics that told of sturdy, white-faced men with sunken eyes who could run long distances, faster than anybody else. They practiced in snow, and their long legs had a circular, high-knee action. They had names like Paavo Nurmi and Ville Ritola, Hannes Kolehmainen, Gunnar Höckert, Lehtinen, Salminen, Iso-Hollo. Some of these modest, quiet men won eight gold medals at the Berlin Olympic Games.

Not long afterward the BBC started featuring Finland in the news bulletins. We had a picture of a small army dressed in white, who would lie facedown in the snow so they were invisible to Russian airplanes. One day one of these men stood up and a Russian fighter plane machine-gunned him. He hid behind a telegraph pole, and the pilot attacked him not once, but five times, from different angles. One bullet hit his gasmask case, but the Finn survived. We were thrilled by these heroics and rushed to our stamp albums to see if Finland had nice stamps.

Suomi-Kuva 1952

The years passed and 1952 approached. Now the whole world had to look to Helsinki, for it had finally achieved its ambition of holding the Olympic Games. The brochures projected more detailed suomi-kuva than those of 1937–1940. Finland was the land of 180,000 lakes, the midnight sun, Lapps, and reindeer. There were no polar bears in the streets but plenty of saunas to protect you against long hard winters, compensated for by short, wonderful summers. The people were depicted as honest, reliable. They meant what they said (if they said anything), worked hard when the money was right, and loved skiing, nature, and fishing through the ice. Men were quiet, fair-haired, and blue-eyed; women were strong-willed, blonde, and beautiful. Finland was not part of the Soviet Union but had good neighborly relations with it. Finland had a democratic constitution and an executive president, just like the U.S.

This image was good enough to encourage foreigners to go and see the Games. We traveled to Stockholm and took the six o'clock evening boat to Turku. There were hundreds of Finns on board and hundreds of other Finns on the quay to see them off. Every single person waved a white handkerchief for twenty minutes as we left. All in dead silence. All you could hear were the cries of sea gulls. We felt we were crossing a new frontier.

Suomi-Kuva 1955 (in Lapland)

A French manager who had spent six months in Finland told the following story: I was skiing with my colleague, Laine, in Lapland. Laine was a good friend but didn't make much conversation. We skied in silence for hours and hours over the Lappish fells. One morning after 2 hours trekking, I saw another skier coming to meet us. He was 15 minutes away. At last I could have a chat. I practiced my miserably few Finnish phrases *"Hyvää paivää. Lumi on hauska tänään. Aurinko paistaa."* He came nearer—half a kilometer, 100 meters, 50 meters—the first phrase was on my lips—then, *swoosh*— he was past and had not said a thing. I was a little bitter about it. I turned to Laine and complained, "That man—he didn't say a word." Laine looked at me and replied, "He was probably from Helsinki. There you have to chatter all the time. He came to Lapland so he wouldn't need to talk to anyone. We don't want to spoil his holiday, do we?"

Suomi-Kuva 1985

An Englishman was hiking round Lapland with his Helsinki friend, Karttunen. One evening they ended up in a small Lappish village, where they had no accommodation, so they decided to walk down the only street to see if anyone would take them in. They said "Hello" to the first three people trudging home in the opposite direction but received nothing more than a curt nod in reply. The fourth person they met, however, responded to Karttunen's hello with a friendly *"Hei"* and a half-smile before continuing on his way. "At least he spoke to us," the Englishman said to Karttunen. "Yes," said his friend, "I knew him quite well at university. We shared the same room together in Helsinki for three years."

Suomi-Kuva 2003

The Finlandia-kuva was alive and well in 2003. I heard the modern version at a dinner in Winchester, England. A British executive there—a Mr. Robinson—on hearing I had lived in Finland, exclaimed, "Oh, I love that country—what marvellous policemen!" Now even after fifty years this was a new one for me, so I asked him to explain to me and the other guests.

Well, I was in this little town of Jämsäkoski," he said. Apparently he was buying paper from his Finnish colleague, Virtanen. In order to impress the Finns, Robinson had driven to Finland in his new Jaguar, which he parked outside the restaurant where Virtanen invited him to dinner. At midnight, after a wonderful meal and half a dozen Koskenkorvas, Virtanen said good night and Robinson had to drive back to his hotel in his Jaguar.

The hotel was on the same street as the restaurant, only 500 meters away. Normally it would have been no problem, but Robinson realized he was very drunk. Should he leave the car in front of the restaurant and walk to the hotel? He thought this would look silly the next morning, so he decided to drive. He drove very slowly, at 5 kilometers per hour. Suddenly, to his horror, he noticed a blue and white car, with a sign "Poliisi," following him. He felt he could do any of three things: (1) stop, get out and walk; (2) continue to drive to the hotel at 5 kilometers per hour; or (3) speed up and drive normally. He decided that the second option was the safest. The police car followed him, at 5 kilometers per hour, to the door of the hotel.

He got out of the car and made his way up the steps of the

hotel entrance. Two policemen got out of the police car and watched him silently. As he opened the hotel door, one of the policemen spoke:

"Good evening, sir."

"Good evening, Officer."

"What is your name and what are you doing in Finland?"

"I'm Robinson from Winchester, England, and I'm buying paper from Mr. Virtanen."

"Oh good. One little point, Mr. Robinson, next time you drive along the main street in Jämsäkoski, would you mind putting your car lights on?"

"Oh thank you Officer, I certainly will."

Robinson turned to enter the hotel, and then the other policeman spoke:

"Just one more thing, Mr. Robinson."

"Yes?"

"In Finland we drive on the right. Good night, sir."

Mr. Robinson, on the basis of this experience, is a loyal ambassador for Finland as he goes about his business in the U.K. Even the police are part of the conspiracy. If this is not brainwashing, what is?

Keeping Suomi-Kuva Alive

The mythology surrounding suomi-kuva is constantly perpetuated by the Finns who live abroad in the form of stories and jokes.

They tell the story about the questionnaire that asked people which end of the bath they sat in. Of the thirty nationalities interviewed, twenty-nine said they sat facing the tap. Only the Finn said he sat the other way, with his back to the tap. Finns are always different. The interviewer was fascinated by this and asked the Finn which atavistic urge or cultural heritage made him sit the wrong way. "Well, I lost the plug," was the reply.

At a dinner in London a Finnish businessman sat explaining to a group of serious listeners why Finland had never established any colonies in Africa. "Well, it all began with the missionaries," he said. Apparently in the early days Finland sent missionaries like everybody else, as these missions eventually led to permanent bases from which colonies emerged. The problem was that many of the missionaries were captured by the Africans. "Just imagine," explained the Finnish informant, "a group of missionaries is caught, consisting of an Englishman, a German, a Frenchman, a Belgian, a Portuguese, and a Finn. The Africans examined each of the prisoners to see which one would make the best meal. And who had the pinkest, most tender flesh after thirty years of sauna? So they ate the Finn first, while some of the others managed to escape.

Martti and Pekka, two middle-aged Finnish peasants, are confirmed bachelors who have built log cabins, five kilometers apart, deep in the forest. They rarely see each other socially, if at all.

One day, Pekka, hearing a knock on his door, opens it and finds Martti there. He lets him in and asks,

"Would you like a cup of coffee?"

"Yes," replies Martti.

Pekka makes coffee and they drink silently for twenty minutes.

"Another cup?" asks Pekka.

"Yes," says Martti.

They drink in silence for another fifteen minutes. When Martti finishes his second cup, Pekka asks,

"What brought you here?"

"My house is on fire," replies Martti.

The Reality for the Visitor

Given the endearing, gutsy, annoying, comical, and darker sides of the Finnish image, what is the foreign visitor to do? Obviously, the

Finns appear different to various nationalities. The Italian finds them wooden, the Spaniard, excessively law-abiding ("They never drive through a red light, even in the middle of the night"). The ultra-polite Japanese see the Finn as a bit rude (without knowing it). A Dane sees them as big drinkers (the women too!), and Swedes often consider them to be slightly dangerous. The British, with their sense of history, see the Finn as David against Goliath, but otherwise fairly normal, though on the quiet side.

Given these different viewpoints, the life of foreigners living and working in Finland is probably what they themselves make it. If they look for the good and the bad, they will probably find both.

You might say the bad is the tight-lipped, so-called winter behavior, which causes Finns to hurry by wordlessly on the street (temperature –20°C) and gulp down their Koskenkorva to thaw out their irritability. Some see Finland as a land full of martyrs, making life difficult for themselves in an already inhospitable corner of Europe. In 1952 there was no alcohol without food, you couldn't have a bath after 11:00 P.M. if you lived in an apartment block, you were not permitted to enter good restaurants unless you wore a formal suit or dress, and the shops usually closed about ten minutes before your working hours allowed you to get to them.

Most of these things have changed, but one still has the worries of prices and taxes being so high that one can hardly breathe. Why do Finns have to build houses of such good quality that you can't afford to pay the rent? Why is the standard of living in Finland so high that most people can't reach it?

At least wages are high, but some foreign managers complain that their employees leave too early in the afternoon, especially when the sun shines. Most Italians, Spaniards, Japanese, and Americans are used to working until 6:00 or 7:00 P.M. Other complaints are about poor communication and absence of any international atmosphere outside Helsinki. However, these things, too, are changing steadily.

But then there is the good. Finnish leadership practices are sound. Finnish managers, like Finnish army officers, usually lead from the front, and they generally strike the right balance between authoritarianism and consultative style.

Although the ice breaks slowly, foreign managers will find that the informal business climate gives them freedom of action. They will not be encumbered by too many manuals, systems, or hierarchical paths, all of which are too common in Germany, France, and the United Kingdom. Finns leave work early, but they start early, and one can have achieved a fine day's work by the time most Britons are heading for lunch and pink gins in their cozy club. Finnish employees are honest, reliable, punctual, and generally loyal. Their sisu qualities are well documented. Bureaucracy, unlike in Germany and France, is kept to a minimum.

Why It's Hard to Stay

The real reasons why foreigners find it difficult to accept long assignments in Finland can be summed up in four points: cost of living, the difficult language, school for children, and the climate. The last two are the most important, for salaries are high and most Finns speak excellent English.

Schooling remains a problem. Most difficult, however, is the ability to accept the rigors of the climate, which are just too much for southern peoples. Italians, Spaniards, and even the French are the hardest hit. One normally enjoys one's first Finnish winter—skiing, the sunsets, and so on. The second is also good, although a bit long. When the third October comes around, though, foreigners start to fancy life in Hawaii. This is also the time when many Finns take a fortnight in the Canaries.

FINNS IN THE NORDIC FRAMEWORK

The director of human resources of a large British company spoke to me recently about intercultural problems resulting from an acquisition they had made. As they had just bought a Finnish firm, I asked him what dissension there was between the Brits and the Finns.

"None at all," he replied, "the problems we are having arise between our Finns and our Swedes."

His remark illustrated a point often made by cross-culturalists—that people with similar cultures run a high risk of misunderstanding each other. Westerners expect the Japanese to be at variance with them on most issues (we often view this variance as engaging, even exotic and refreshing). By the same token, we are prepared and make provision for the contrastive doctrines and precepts of Islam when our social or business activities bring us into contact with Arabs. We often fail to make the same allowances, however, when dealing with cultures close to our own. Because our neighbors (or racial cousins) may share our religion, laws, customs, sense of time, and other surface values, we tend to get irritated when they deviate from this common path. Thus, English people, who cheerfully acknowledge the use of chopsticks by the Chinese or the Arab custom of eating by hand, find it quite strange when they see Americans cut their meat with their knife, then put it by their plate, change the fork from the left hand to the right, and eat one-handed with the left shoulder dipped.

We tend to make even fewer concessions when the other culture uses the same language. If Americans speak English, think the Brits, why don't they exercise the subtle humor, understatement, and adroit verbal restraint that affords the English so much social dexterity? The magniloquent Americans, on the other hand—given to hyperbole as a route to clarity, may be forgiven for thinking the British are close-mouthed, verbally opaque, and, at the worst, darn devious.

In the Nordic area the three Scandinavian languages are so close that Swedes, Norwegians, and Danes inevitably each feel that the other two languages are rather odd dialects of their own. This perceived oddness may then be subconsciously transferred to the individual speaking the language. Why should a Norwegian say "three-and-fifty," thinks the Swede, when he could perfectly well say "fifty-three"?

Finnish, as we have learned, is very different from Scandinavian languages, so this type of linguistic prejudgment does not occur. The uncompromising, esoteric impact of the Finnish language puts the Scandinavians—as indeed many others—in their place. That is to say, a cultural divide is established, decisively and enduringly. A kind of ethnic statement has been made—we, the Finns, live in these parts with you Scandinavians, but we have different aesthetics and a different world outlook; it is evident in our language, music, literature, sense of color, and sensitivities.

Historical propinquity has encouraged the Nordic nations to assume, in moments of forgetfulness, that they share an identical world outlook. Then they get irritated with each other when they find they do not. This disputatiousness is by no means limited to Finns and Swedes. The grievances and vexations Swedes and Norwegians have with each other are only too well known.

The Swedish Connection

Because of Swedish and Finnish shared history and their sizable shared border, the relationship between these two countries warrants particular attention. Between Finland and Sweden there is an enduring feeling of competition or contest. Finland—not Denmark or Norway—is Sweden's rival for Nordic limelight. The annual athletic meets between the two countries are always a tense, passionate occasion, and the parallel encounters in ice hockey and other winter sports feature just as much flag waving. Finland's substantial land area, her strategic geographical location, her proud war record, her still-fresh independence, and her recent decade of economic boom all make her Sweden's big cousin, to be reckoned with in the Nordic family.

The mutual sense of competition arises not from a lack of acceptance of each other's differences, for the Swedes see the Finns as friendly, but as exotic, anomalous, and often impenetrable. The friction that occurs between the two peoples arises from their similarity. Finns, notwithstanding their only-too-obvious uniqueness, are more "Scandinavian" than they realize. In the first place, Finnish history, both in the sense of social interaction and political destiny, was closely intertwined with that of Sweden for over six hundred years, as explained in Chapter 4. During this long period many Swedish customs and institutions established themselves firmly in Finland. Often the process was less a handed-down edict than a new development in a shared nation. Lutheranism, social justice, respect for education, aversion to violence, and social stability feature in Finnish attitudes and outlook as strongly as they do in Swedish.

Secondly, many Finns have a good proportion of Swedish blood in their veins, particularly those living in southwestern Finland and along the Gulf of Bothnia. This has resulted in considerable similarity in appearance as well as the development of certain common mannerisms and modes of expression.

Extensive Finnish immigration to Sweden in the 1950s and 1960s and substantial cross-investment between Swedish and Finnish companies have led to an enormous increase in business and social contacts between the two peoples. Intercultural contact does not, however, always lead to intercultural understanding. Few countries have such close and long-standing cultural exchanges as England and France, yet these peoples misunderstand each other frequently. Probably, Swedes and Finns get on with each other better than do the English and the French, but beware—things don't always go smoothly! Questionnaires put to Finns and Swedes regarding what they think of each other are far from reassuring.

Finns, asked to select eight adjectives from a list to describe themselves, came up on average with the following: honest, slow, reliable, true, shy, direct, reserved, and punctual. When they were asked to pick eight adjectives from the same list, for the Swedes, they chose snobbish, weak-willed, caring, boring, serious, collective, sociable, and polite. Not a completely unfavorable judgment but hardly flattering!

Swedes, using the same list, described themselves as honest, punctual, efficient, not comfortable with taking risks, lacking social confidence, serious, strong technically, and polite.

We have said earlier that Finns are extremely interested in cultural relativism, leading to a high degree of national self-consciousness and the ability to see themselves. Swedes, according to Laine Sveiby, evidently are not so blessed. It follows that Finns devote more thought to the cultural relationship between Finland and Sweden than do the Swedes. But too much analysis and generalizing can be dangerous, leading to entrenched negative stereotyping. For instance,

1. Finns think Swedes are too formal,
2. Finns think Swedes think Finns are too rustic,
3. Finns think Swedes think they (the Swedes) are technically the most advanced, and
4. Finns think that Swedes think that Finns think Swedes are snobbish.

Only in the first instance can Finns judge matters with some confidence, and even here it is a question of relativity. Considering the other three, we are dealing of course with speculation, since how can Finns *really* know what Swedes think of them? Do Swedes in reality have such a negative view of Finnish people? My own direct questioning of Swedes regarding their opinion of Finns elicited widely differing responses, ranging from very negative to laudatory. The pattern that emerged was that the more a Swede knows about the Finns, the more positive the view becomes. Some descriptions follow, based on the amount of contact the Swede has with the Finn:

- Mr. A (rarely meets Finns): Pale-skinned and blond-haired, like sauna, drinking, and fighting with knives.
- Mr. B (rarely meets Finns): Dark and melancholy, brood too much, rather dull.
- Mr. C (meets Finns occasionally): Men more boring than the women, seemingly a question of Finnish men's inhibitions.
- Mr. D (meets Finns regularly): Silent but have improved a lot over the last ten years.
- Mr. E (meets Finns regularly): Women are more open, even aggressive, smart and well-dressed, without being *chic*.
- Mr. F (regular contact with Finns): Quiet people but hard-working, competent, and well educated; don't bother you with small talk, but get on with their job and bring you the results in due course.
- Mr. G (regular contact with Finns): Difficult to get to know them; are shy, reserved, but kind; once inside their protective armor, you are quite pleased with what you find.
- Mr. H (daily contact with Finns): Quietly ambitious, diligent, and quite demanding at times; (You must keep your word!) I love working with them, but I never know what they really think.

- Mr. I (daily contact with Finns): Finns don't give enough feedback; we never know whether they are satisfied or not, but they are never unfair in their judgment; they are to be trusted.
- Mr. J (works for Finnish company in Sweden): They think in isolation and feed you information on a need-to-know basis; Finns, though, will (eventually) tell you if they think something is good or bad.
- Mr. K (works for Finnish company): Very well educated, not afraid to make decisions; speak more slowly than Swedes, but I suspect they think faster.
- Mr. L (lived in Finland two years): Finns are well educated with a high demand for competence and knowledge. Businessmen often have advanced academic degrees, and many secretaries are extremely well qualified. They call themselves secretaries, but they are actually high-class female executives. Finns are more humble than Swedes when first meeting strangers, and many Swedes find them buttoned up. Actually, I think it is misleading. Swedes seem to have more social ease at first but are really quite "buttoned up" inside. Once you have unbuttoned a Finn you find clear thinking and straightforward attitudes "inside." They make decisions faster than Swedes do. If they make a wrong decision, they will accept responsibility for it and sort out the problem later. Swedes are far more cautious and must examine all pertinent details first. Swedes in general know very little about the Finns. Those who have lived in Finland come back with a very positive impression.

The point about differences in decision making is important and is frequently commented on by businesspeople of both nationalities. Laine Sveiby opines that Finns are more spontaneous making decisions and more confident among themselves than Swedes are. Their individualism encourages them to shy away from "collectively accepted myths." Swedes, on their side, are uncomfortable with the Finns' more authoritative style.

Finns and Swedes share some of the same strengths: ability to listen well, desire to learn, honest endeavour, loyalty, long-term thinking, and attention to quality. These common traits are the basis of cooperation between Swedes and Finns, which in general is quite good. However, constant consultation at all levels in the Swedish company, endless meetings, habitual deferment of final decisions, obsession with people orientation, difficulties in firing incompetent employees, ultra-cautiousness, and no little dithering are sources of frustration for Finnish managers in Sweden (and for other nationalities, too).

Sweden, a Black Sheep in the Neighborhood

In the world at large, and especially in the English-speaking world, the Swedes seem to be universally popular. Their clean-cut profile as honest, caring, well-informed, efficient plodders, producing quality goods delivered on time, sits well with their frequently well-groomed appearance, good sense of dress, and (forgive the stereotyping) blond hair and blue eyes. Their English, grammatically proficient, is clean and crisp, like that of Scots who went to Oxford. In society set pieces, at least, they have impeccable manners and say all the right things for the first fifteen minutes.

The Swedes don't fare nearly as well in their own neighborhood. They are unpopular and often ridiculed throughout the Nordic area. The fact that none of the Swedes' neighbors—Denmark, Norway, Finland—have any undue reputation for aggressiveness makes the antipathy all the more unexpected. What, in fact, is wrong with the Swedes? This is a question that the Swedes themselves have been trying to answer over the last few decades.

In the first place, all four countries are neighbors: neighborly love is not a human characteristic. Around the globe perhaps only the Canadians and the Americans share a long border with a minimum of animosity. Further, Norway, Denmark, and Finland are less impressed than others by the splendor of the Swedish welfare state; they have similar creations of their own (and there is a growing doubt in all four countries that the system will really work in the very long run). Their cynicism vis-à-vis Sweden also has historical underpinnings:

- Denmark was for a long period a major player in the area (it colonized Norway for 400 years).
- Swedes often laid siege to Copenhagen.
- **Swedes ruled Finland for 600 years.**
- Sweden and Norway shared an uncomfortable union until 1905.
- Norway, Denmark, and especially Finland were battered in the Second World War. Sweden was not.

Swedish industry enjoyed a period of prosperity in the years from 1945 to 1960, when Norway and Denmark got off to a much slower post-war start and Finland was badly handicapped with repaying huge (and unfair) war reparations to the Russians (1945–1952). The big Swedish multinationals—Volvo, Saab, Electrolux, SKF, Axel Johnson, and so on—boomed during these years, when Swedish steel was reputedly the best in the world and the "Flying Barrel" was a leading fighter plane. Others' prosperity often gives rise to neighbors' envy, especially when accompanied by a certain complacency. In the Nordic zone, Sweden was seen as big, export-minded, financially strong, well-fed, and irritatingly smug.

The Finns do not know the Norwegians, Danes, and Icelanders very well, but they like them more. Annual surveys show quite clearly that Finns consistently rate Norwegians as the most popular foreigners. They feel that the two peoples share several characteristics, including honesty, straight talk, dry humor, deliberation, endurance, obstinacy, love of solitude, and aversion to Swedes. Actual contact between Finns and Norwegians in day-to-day activity is quite limited, as their common frontier is well up in the Arctic, and mountains provide a formidable barrier. Finns have good things to say about Danes, though they recognize that they are less like Finns than are the Swedes, since they generally have few inhibitions about conversing freely and are sometimes seen as a trifle slick. In fact, Finns trust Swedes more than they think they do.

Finns know little about Icelanders, except again they "like" them, though the sheep and fish economy of the latter offers little common ground for the more industrialized Finns. In fact, drinking habits in Iceland strongly resemble those of rural Finland.

Conclusion

In the field of Nordic cooperation, which has a successful history, Finland feels very much at home and is completely accepted as a member of the group by all the others, even though her language and origins are different. Though Finns have blood relations elsewhere—Estonians, Hungarians, Ingermanlanders, and so on—their feeling of "belonging" to the Scandinavian group is stronger. Not only do Finns have a generous ratio of Swedish blood, but the customs union and the smoothly functioning Nordic Council have strengthened the fraternal feelings for their neighbors in the west. Similarities in social progress and justice are striking in all five Nordic countries. The GDP per head is more or less on a par across the five nations. All have approximately the same purchasing power, allowing for some variances in the respective economies. All five countries rate high on the Human Development Index, have achieved among the lowest infant mortality rates, are the world's most literate people (99 percent), and have the smallest households. Laws, social security, standards of hygiene, judicial procedures, education systems, and police practices resemble each other across the board, while the common interest in winter sports in Finland, Norway, and Sweden further cements the Nordic relationship. Above all, the five countries settle their differences by means of that essentially Nordic ingredient—common sense. It is an admirable substitute for too much talk.

FINNS AND OTHERS

In general the Finns, like other Nordics, enjoy a universally cred-
itable reputation as straightforward players and solid citizens, and
are known for clean living. Swedes and Norwegians in particular
are grateful for having Finland as their eastern neighbor, especially
when they consider the alternative.

In view of their eastern origins, it is nothing short of remarkable
how snugly the Finnish mindset dovetails with Anglo-Saxon cultures. The Finns fought the Russians to defend (their) democracy,
and they always pay their debts. That is a lot in Anglo-Saxon eyes.
Finnish adoption of Protestant ethics gives them a strong identity
with New World emigrants of Northern European origin. This
applies not only to the U.S. but also to Canadians, Australians, New
Zealanders, and South Africans. Australians would like Finns to be
a bit more "matey," but they say the same thing about the British.
The more conservative New Zealanders and South Africans find the
Finns just right. Canadians and Britons quickly find the Finns'
wavelength and appreciate their humor.

The French, the Italians, and the Spanish

The French live in a world of their own, the center of which is
France. They are immersed in their own history and tend to believe

that France has set the norms for such things as democracy, justice, governmental and legal systems, military strategy, philosophy, science, agriculture, viniculture, haute cuisine, and savoir faire in general. Other nations, according to the French, vary from these norms and have a lot to learn before they get things right.

The French know virtually nothing about Finland; their educational system teaches little of the history or geography of the small nations, and those who have not lived in Finland rarely penetrate the suomi-kuva smoke screen of saunas, lakes, forests, and Lapps. Most French people think Finland, like Poland and Hungary, is "East European," and when the Iron Curtain disappeared, they believed that the Finns had emerged from behind it. The general French attitude toward Finns is pleasant enough, neither positive nor negative. They are strangers from a small, new, rather distant land; they speak a difficult language (which they think is Scandinavian), have come from the cold, and appear rather cold to them. They will do business with Finns if they have a good product, or if they want to buy from the French, but their initial posture will be somewhat condescending. Finns do not speak French, and they appear to be Anglophiles. That is not a good start in French eyes.

French companies with a history of trading with Finland and those French people who work for Finnish companies in France (e.g., Kone) are much better informed and see Finns as serious and competitive businesspeople. They are not, however, seen as equals. They may be better or worse, but they are different. The French, like the Japanese, believe they are unique and do not really expect that others will ever be able to completely conform to their standards.

When dealing with the French, Finns have to behave much more formally than they usually do, using only surnames and showing almost exaggerated politeness to French senior executives. At the same time, Finns have to appear "more human" than usual; the French are, after all, Latins in spite of their logic and exactness. The French like a good discussion and observe few time limits when in the midst of one. If Finns don't talk enough, the French will call them monosyllabic afterward. Finns need to stick to logic at all times, avoiding American-style "hunches" or British-style "feel for situations." The French pounce on contradictions.

If the French find Finns monosyllabic, the Italians see them as wooden, probably boring, certainly very uncommunicative. We are dealing with two extremes, the most introverted and the most extroverted of European peoples. Italians, at ease with other Latins, find even the Germans and British rather opaque. They have strategies for flattering them and "softening them up." With a Finn, the ploy does not work. The more expressive and persuasive the Italian is, the more withdrawn and suspicious the Finn appears. Why can't he be more human, communicative, and flexible—like an Italian? Thank God, the women are better! But what a climate! Brrr . . .

A few years ago, I was visiting the historic town of Agrigento in Sicily with a charming Sicilian banker, Francesco Ingrassia, and a somewhat less charismatic Finnish consultant, Jarmo Jyrkinen. As Francesco, our host, was showing us around, it began to rain, just a little. "Jarmo," exclaimed Francesco, "it's raining!"

Jarmo looked at him stonily. "I can see that it is raining," he replied.

"Imagine, Jarmo, it is raining in Agrigento!" shouted Francesco.

"I don't have to imagine anything," retorted Jarmo. "I know when it is raining on me."

"Yes, but in Agrigento in July!" continued our Italian host.

"Francesco, I know this town's name. I know we are in the month of July. Why do you have to tell me all this?" I felt sorry for Francesco, the most sociable of human beings.

Spaniards visiting Finland have similar impressions—Finnish males have no body language or charisma; they seem cold and unmovable. Finns visiting Spain find some variety in their reception: there is only one Finland, but there are several Spains, dating back to the Romans. Castilians are in the majority and continue to dominate, but depending on a Spaniard's origins, doing business with Finns may hold varied promises and challenges.

- Galicians are practical and melancholy, sharing some common ground with the Finns.
- Aragonese stubbornness finds an echo in Finnish sisu.
- Basques have a talent for industry and commerce and, along with Finns, Hungarians, and Estonians, they have no Indo-European ancestry. The synthetic nature of their language in some respects resembles Finnish.
- Catalans, who face France rather than Spain, share the cult of efficiency with Finns.

Finns will find they have little in common with two other regions.

- Asturians, who are extremely haughty, share few characteristics with Finns.
- Andalucians appear to be orators, and timetables are for cats and dogs—also traits the Finns don't share.

Castilians and Finns are a poor mix. The former are basically Latins, and indeed for many centuries they were the guardians of the Roman heritage, preserving its linguistic and literary monuments as well as its traditions of conquest and empire. Latin characteristics evident in Castile are verbosity and eloquence. (The Castilian word *hablar*—"to speak"—comes from *fabulare,* meaning "to invent, to romance, to revel in the joys of conversation.") Finns will hardly feel comfortable confronted by such wordiness, nor with the Spaniards' favorite role, the supreme romantic. Proud of their history, Castilians are at heart crusaders, mystic, impractical individualists who were supreme as conquistadors but were notably unable to organize their empire. Finns may admire Castilian individualism, since it is a trait they cherish, but individualism in Spain has resulted in unruliness toward authority and organization, even scorn for government. In Spain, Finns are seen as law-abiding, to the point of being docile.

If the orderly Finns find this distrust of authority hard to swallow, they will be even more perplexed with Castilian fatalism. Why try to direct our fate so much? says the Castilian—all that happens now has happened before and will certainly happen again. Tomorrow is another day; if it is our destiny to succeed, we shall. The Finns, who shrugged off Russian fatalism and consider themselves masters of their own fate, have little sympathy for this attitude. Finns insist that facts are stubborn things, but Spaniards assert that things are not what they seem: there is a double truth, that of the immediate detail and that of the poetic whole. The second is more important for the Castilian, because it supplies a faith or vision to live by. One must realize the futility of material ambition.

It should be fairly clear by now that the Spaniard and the Finn have quite different perceptions of reality. Dialogue between the two is never going to be easy. A grandiloquent, circumlocutory orator addresses a passive listener. The supreme romanticists expound their views to the taciturn pragmatist. There will probably also be a language barrier. Yet dialogue there must be, in the world of business.

A Finn has to work hard to make a Spaniard like him. Finns must show that they have a heart and that they do not take everything seriously. Finns have big hearts, but they are experts at keeping them well hidden. A Finn will need to talk to a Spaniard with a twinkle in his eye and thump him on the back when somebody tells a joke. *Macho* is a Spanish word, and the essential masculinity of the Finn stands him in good stead in a Spaniard's company. Finnish businesswomen will be comfortable with male Spaniards, as their relative aggressiveness will score points, and no doubt their blonde good looks will not go unnoticed.

When conversing with a Spaniard, it is best for Finns to shed some of their monochronic tendencies: forget the dictates of time, admit that some roguery actually exists in Finland, confess to a few private sins or misdemeanors, ask some rather personal questions, stay up drinking together until three in the morning, and in general let their hair down. Protestant values must be temporarily discarded during the conversation.

Other Europeans

Finland has a very comfortable relationship with both Germany and Britain. These two countries, along with Sweden, are the main destinations for Finnish exports as well as the principal origins of Finnish imports. The substantial reciprocal trade means that both Germans and Britons have an increasing number of contacts with Finns as the latter seek a bigger share of Western markets. Germans recognize in Finns many of their own qualities—honesty, frankness, punctuality, solid workmanship, and a kind of Arctic *Gründlichkeit* (thoroughness). All classes of British like Finns, though the world-view resemblance is strongest among the northern English and the Scots.

Finns are viewed in a positive light in Holland and in the Flemish portion of Belgium, but south of Brussels the image changes. French-speaking Belgians are less impressed by Protestant values, many of which they consider pedantic, unimaginative, and misguided.

As for the Russians, Finland and Russia have gone to war ten times, and the total Russian dead on the Finnish front between 1939 and 1944 was over 400,000. In spite of this, the people like each other. Although a certain type of Finn spits out the word *venaläiset* (Russians) in the same way he would deliver an oath, the object of his venom is in nearly all cases the concept of the malignant Russian state rather than the individual. The Finns see the average Russian as a warm-hearted, sentimental, rather uncivilized creature, but they do not feel he or she is malicious or anti-Finnish. Russians corroborate this; they have a warm feeling toward Finns, whose bravery, society, and technology they admire. In spite of their many battles, Russians see Finns as neighbors who pose no threat. This did not prevent them taking a big slice of Finland's territory in 1944 and imposing crippling war reparations, but Stalin at least did not demand total capitulation. It is said he had a soft spot for Finland. (Who knows?)

Most Portuguese know very little about Finns. When I questioned a group of Lisbon businessmen recently about Finnish characteristics, they were only aware of one of the Finnish "virtues"—that concerning Finland's record in sports. Mexicans and South Americans have only a vague idea where Finland is. The other half-Latins—the Romanians—do not get on well with Finns, who regard them as quite unreliable in business. In a recent survey Finns listed Serbs as the most unpopular Europeans. Greeks have little to do with Finland; Turks, surprisingly, are both knowledgeable about and fond of Finns, with whom they claim kinship. The roaring trade they do with Finns in leather jackets in the resorts of Bodrum and Marmaris may have something to do with this outpouring of affection.

The Hungarians, we can safely assume, *are* related to the Finns, and are proud of their northern cousins, distant though they are. As we creep up back again toward the Baltic, Czechs and Poles both admire Finland and welcome Finns both as tourists and as business partners. People from the Baltic states have slightly varying attitudes. Each one of them envies Finland's having secured her independence in 1944 and would wish to emulate her economic success in the eastern Baltic. Catholic Lithuania, however, traditionally faces Poland. Protestant Latvians, with their orderliness and reserve, tend to look toward Sweden and Finland for guidance and inspiration. The Estonians, closely related to the Finns both racially and linguistically (many Estonians speak almost perfect Finnish), definitely have the Finnish model in close focus. The frequent ferries between Helsinki and Tallinn are generally full in both directions.

Africans and Arabs

Sub-Saharan Africans have little in common with the Finns as far as mental programming is concerned, and few Africans come to Finland to stay. Finland's intake of 2,800 Somalis after 1990, on humanitarian grounds, cannot be described as a success.

Finnish qualities and values are almost diametrically opposed to those of the Arabs of North Africa and the Middle East. Traditional Arab rhetoric falls on deaf ears in Finland. Arabs consider that when people speak in a low voice, they are insincere or do not really mean what they say. When they stand nearer to Finns to get the message, the Finns back away. (Do I smell?) Finns appear to Arabs as detached, impersonal, and unwilling to mention even Finnish achievements or strengths. They seem to be reluctant to either accept or accord favors. The typical Arab, only too ready to boast of his connections, demonstrates his willingness to make them available to people he makes friends with. He is bewildered by the cool impartiality of the Finns in this respect. The strong position of Finnish women is also confusing.

The only favorable impressions Finns make on Arabs is their high level of education and technical expertise, apart from exhibiting considerably less arrogance than representatives of such larger nations as France and Britain.

Asians

In Asia, Finns are understood better than they are in many countries. As their communication style is basically Asiatic (see Chapter 7), they are well accepted by the Japanese, who like their quietness, modesty, and nonverbal skills. Although Finns often upset the Japanese by being too frank and direct, or by shaking hands too hard, in general Finnish and Japanese businesspeople get on very well, as there is usually an early realization of mutual trust. Japanese are culturally very different from all other peoples, but there is some truth in the view that Finns resemble the Japanese more than do any other Europeans.

Finns who live in Japan are quick to notice several striking similarities between the Finnish and Japanese languages. Though these resemblances are to some extent superficial, Finns find Japanese easy to pronounce (*Yokohama-koko-kana*) and are intrigued by

Finn-friendly vocabulary items such as *uma* (*humma*), *matsu* (*mänty*), *fune* (*vene*), *isu* (*istuin*), *juoparatte* (*juopporatti* or *juoppo-ralli*), even the question-forming *-ka* (*-ko* or *-kö*). These "friends" do not enable Finns to understand Japanese any more than they do Hungarian, but the fact that these words find an echo only in Finnish among languages spoken in Europe triggers a slight feeling of kinship between the two peoples. This is quickly strengthened by the realization that speaking a "unique" language is a feeling shared strongly by both Finns and Japanese. Both experience a sense of isolation from groups that have many cousins (Germans, Britons, Swedes, or French, Italians, Portuguese). This sense of isolation results in a feeling of specialness and with it a heightening of the national self-consciousness.

The Japanese think well of Finland. They are pleased to observe that the Finns, like they, do not appreciate being touched or hugged, and the "distance of comfort" between two Finnish speakers is approximately the same as in Japan (about 1.2 m).

Both countries share a common neighbor (the Russian Federation) and are keenly conscious of its size and pressure. Both have been greatly influenced culturally by another neighbor (China, in the case of Japan, and Sweden, in the Finnish case) and occasionally display a slight inferiority complex in this regard. Yet both Japan and Finland have excelled in the arts and take pride in this.

The sense of isolation due to geographical location and strangeness of language leads both Finns and Japanese to believe that they are poor at learning foreign languages, and this sometimes discourages them from trying to speak much, as they do not wish to make mistakes. Neither people likes losing face.

Japanese durability and stamina are matched by Finnish sisu, and both peoples are formidable in war, though now both are dedicated to preserving the peace. The same common tenacity has helped both nations attain economic success after military defeats—Japan's export-driven miracle has been matched by high Finnish living standards.

Because both Finns and Japanese consider themselves to be poor at verbal communication (and this is probably true, if we compare them with French or Americans), they have developed nonverbal skills to a high degree. The Japanese is extremely polite and considerate and shows this in nonverbal ways such as body language, gentleness, and gift giving. The Finn achieves communication through quiet but obvious friendliness, cozy silences, inviting gestures, shy kindness, sauna sharing, and offering excellent coffee or something stronger to keep out the cold. Japanese (themselves hot-bath lovers) delight in these quiet offerings, shared silences, and controlled sociability. Groups of Finns and Japanese with no common language have no difficulty socializing comfortably for hours, whereas Swedes and Spaniards (or Portuguese and Germans) find it less easy.

Koreans have a similar attitude, even appreciating Finnish directness. The Chinese approve of Finnish tranquility and sincerity and respect their record of paying bills quickly. On the whole, Finns are good European ambassadors in Asia, where self-effacement and patience often carry the day.

U.S. Americans

Which leaves us with the U.S. Americans. Americans like Finns, and Finns like Americans. Surveys carried out by Finnish government departments show that Finns consistently rate Americans as the third most popular nationality (after the Norwegians and British and way ahead of Swedes, Germans, and Latins). Tens of thousands of Finns have emigrated to the United States and prospered there. Settling in areas that bear a strong topographical resemblance to Finland (Minnesota, Wisconsin, Michigan, etc.), they have proven to be diligent, dutiful, equable citizens, adapting easily to American life. In the dynamic, often disputatious framework of cosmopolitan American society, they have distinguished themselves by their unpretentiousness. In American eyes, they have played the game.

It is only natural that when Finland secured her long-awaited independence in 1917, the shining model of American democracy should loom large in the new national consciousness. America—the land of the free—championed the small, the poor, and the brave. Finland was all of these and had had a war of independence to boot. Her constitution drew heavily on American inspiration, particularly the power and activity of the office of the president. In her brief history Finland has been fortunate in her choice of presidents, several of whom have personified the resilience and rugged independence of the nation.

Well before independence, Finland and her people had acquired and assimilated many characteristics that would sit well with the adventurous descendants of the early American colonists. Christianity came to Finland early. More than 90 percent of Finns are officially Lutheran, and the Protestant work ethic and the right to dissent were core values for them in the same way as they were for the Virginians and their successors. During many centuries of Swedish and Russian domination, Finns consistently displayed, sometimes fiercely, an indomitable, independent nature.

In spite of their long-standing familiarity with Russians and Swedes, independent Finns have looked to England and the United States with eager eyes and a growing sense of affinity. Neither Scandinavian nor Slavic in origin, Finns lean (consciously and subconsciously) toward Anglo-Saxon individualism, humor, casualness, and freedom of expression. In the American pioneer, particularly, Finns saw many of their own native traits—the direct approach, ready informality, use of first names, indifference to titles or aristocratic pedigree, aversion to stuffiness or snobbery, self-reliance, and (when required) unquestioned bravery.

The American frontiersman had shown toughness and tenacity, which equated with Finnish sisu. Close to nature and often alone, he developed determination to survive, as many a Finn had before him. Both have a problem-solving streak, preferably in isolation. Both stick to what has been agreed.

Finns and Americans in the Workplace

In business, Finns and Americans share many common goals and ideas. Business is based on punctuality, solid figures, proven techniques, pragmatic reasoning, and technical competence. Both peoples are low context, preferring to gather information from established sources. Common sense and reliability are expected and usually demonstrated. Americans find their own frankness, self-reliance, and tenacity mirrored in the Finnish psyche. Finns, like Americans, believe that all are created equal; any form of snobbery or pulling rank is abhorrent. Informality of discourse, egalitarian address, and a minimum of protocol typify Finnish/American meetings. Humor can play an important part in cementing empathy.

While many traits are similar, there are, however, considerable differences as well. In terms of communication, egalitarianism may dominate, but Finns are, as you already know, much more introverted than Americans. In the United States time is money, and the American wishes to get the deal done in the shortest time possible. This leads him to be frequently impatient, occasionally aggressive. Finns, by nature, are essentially patient and trained to curb aggressiveness, even open displays of feeling.

Americans see nothing wrong with extroversion; they are open, frank, and have nothing to hide. Finns, while valuing frank discussion, are careful about revealing their soul. Americans are talkative and persuasive. Finns are reticent, often silent, and trained not to force their opinions on others. If they disagree, they will often remain silent. Americans cannot stand silence during meetings, so they often take the Finn's turn to speak (with the best of intentions, wishing to be more explicit and helpful). Finns, who distrust verbosity, may then go into their shell. Americans, used to open debate and give-and-take argument, will often interrupt a Finn when the latter finally decides to speak. This breaks a sacred rule for a Finn, who is taught from infancy not to interrupt.

American persuasiveness often leads to hyperbole, again with the best of intentions (where the American is trying to show the desirability of the deal). This conflicts with the Finnish tendency toward understatement and modesty. Americans, proud of their company's success or of their country, may innocently indulge in laudatory statements that the Finn sees as outright boasting. American businesspeople enter a meeting with a broad smile on their face, even for complete strangers. Finns enter first meetings unsmiling, as do Germans and Russians. Coaxing smiles out of Finns can be a two-hour task, unless you have some good stories. Finns find both American and Japanese smiles insincere.

Americans and Finns differ in their approach to supervision in the workplace. It has been mentioned earlier that Finnish workers or clerical staff do not like being monitored, followed around, interfered with, or even praised when they are doing the job. American managers who pop their head around a Finnish assistant's door with remarks like "Say, Paavo, I've just had a great idea" or "Need any help?" only make nuisances of themselves if they do this frequently. Finnish women are less resentful—they maintain an inquiring stance when contemplating the workings of the mind of the foreigner, especially males—but Finnish men, particularly, hate disturbance once the directive has been properly issued. They wish to concentrate single-mindedly on the task in hand and, in fact, do it *their* way.

Americans working on interesting projects tend to maintain a constant dialogue with each other during the process. They pace up and down, think aloud, and welcome brainstorming when they can make it happen. Finns, by contrast, indulge in unilateral brainstorming, at a slower pace, but in considerable depth. Finns are not averse to teamwork in principle, but it is achieved by meeting periodically to show and compare the results of work that has already been carried out individually—and in their own corner.

Finns, like Americans, are great problem solvers—they enjoy both the challenge posed by difficulties and the satisfaction of surmounting hurdles. Americans solve problems more quickly than

Finns do. Americans are impatient with their problems; Finns are patient with theirs. This difference sometimes causes a conflict, as the Finns react against being pushed toward a solution. They are more often perfectionist than the Americans, who are realistic enough but see life as short and are anxious to achieve a quota of attainments in a given time frame. Finnish perfectionism can be likened to that of the Germans in their goal of a perfectly ordered world or the Japanese in their quest for a zero-defect production. A Finn, like a German, guards constantly against leaving him- or herself open to criticism for earlier neglect or carelessness.

Conflict resolution is another area where Americans must tread carefully when on Finnish soil. Americans should bear in mind that rank may not be pulled, seniority may not replace logic, and bulldozing is out of the question when opinions collide. One of the most frequently heard questions emanating from foreign managers is "How do you get Finns to change their mind when they have taken a stand?" The answer to this question is that it is invariably difficult, is often impossible, and should rarely be attempted. Conflict with Finns is best avoided at any early stage. Once attitudes have hardened, Finns are among the most intransigent of people. On the other hand, they are most cooperative when their creative abilities are quickly recognized. It is not praise they seek but the early integration of their original ideas in the planning of a project. They must see themselves in it. When this is the case, they do not wish to dominate. Conflict will not occur if Finns are asked in the planning stage what they think about things and what they can contribute. They are not Japanese waiting for orders; they are fertile thinkers within Finnish conditions. American managers, having asked for Finnish advice, should then wait the time it takes to get an answer. It will be unhurried but well thought out and, frequently, appropriate. Finns, on the other hand, will be eager to enter into conflict with people who try to best them with brute force, devious methods, or, worst of all, an overdose of charisma.

Differences in communication style between Finns and Americans do not, however, erect permanent barriers, though they can be disconcerting in the initial stages of contact. Soon each side perceives that a large amount of trust and goodwill will emanate from the dealings. Finns come to realize that the Americans, used to formulating get-to-know-you-quick strategies for greeting strangers, are not especially keen on deceiving the Finns with their instant friendliness. On the other hand, Americans soon see that Finnish reticence and gloomy expressions conceal hearts of gold.

The Finns, too, have a lot of cards up their sleeve and possess certain traits that may complicate the relationship. Though they are, in general, modest and not chauvinistic, they have an inner, deeply rooted conviction that Finnish norms are optimal. These include a sense of ultra-honesty, hatred of debt, true friendship, unswerving reliability, and perfection of workmanship. Their sense of separateness from other peoples, their lingering uneasiness in the presence of foreigners, their hidden contempt for verbosity lead them frequently to be judgmental. They admire the American frontier spirit without reservation: the entrepreneurial attitude, the risk taking, the mobility and opportunism, the luring path from rags to riches.

The breakneck pace of American life is another matter. The reflective Finn prizes unhurried calm. Okay, time is money, but single-minded pursuit of wealth conflicts with Finnish ideas about self-fulfillment, artistic goals, calm inventiveness, and concern with the environment. And why are Americans so desperate for popularity? Why do they long so much to be stars, to receive acclaim? Why do junior executives need constant praise and pep talks from their supervisors? A Finn just gets on with the job, monitoring him- or herself in the process. Why are Americans so suspicious of intellectuals and openly distrustful of "eggheads"? Has recognition of dollar status somehow clouded perceptions of scholastic and moral values? And what about the spread of crime in the United States?

Finns are not particularly litigious; they are apprehensive about the number of lawyers required to mediate U.S. disputes, not to mention the astronomic sums involved. Whenever possible, Finns avoid a fuss. They see Americans as media-driven, not thinking enough for themselves. Finns, too, are great readers of newspapers (and books) but consider their press well-balanced and playing down sensationalism. Americans have no great aversion to exaggeration, as they are future-orientated optimists who like to think big. Finns are practiced (selective) pessimists; they think in niches.

The cautiously critical Finnish view of American "excesses" does not result in anti-Americanism—far from it. Like the British, Finns see Americans as big, generous, genial friends (British would say cousins) who have had the mantle of world leadership thrust upon them, often botch it up (as others did before them), and fall prey to European cynicism and Asian competition. The Finn sees the American as a valued partner and friend whom he or she openly admires but secretly considers needful of Finnish balance and tranquility.

Solid and nonsimplistic, Finns know more about the big nations than the latter know about Finland. They have seen our films, read our books, studied our histories, and learned our languages. They have widened their horizons when often we have not (see Figure 11.1). Americans, like the French, are openly messianic. They will save the world for democracy and free trade while the French will civilize us. Finns, though nonmessianic on the surface, have a silent program. They have not yet stated their manifesto, but the more they internationalize, the surer they are that they have something to teach the rest of us. We may do well to listen.

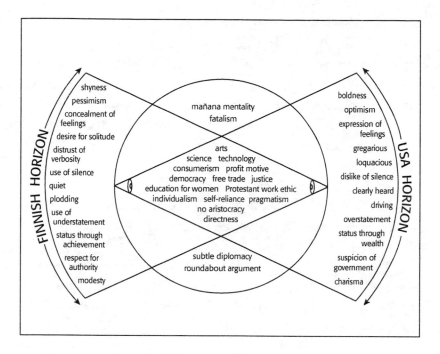

FIGURE 11.1   Finnish and U.S. Horizons

Negotiating with and Motivating Finns

When managing or entering into negotiations with Finns, foreign managers should note the following Finnish negotiating characteristics and procedures:

- Informality: first names are used quickly, and jackets may be taken off soon.
- Egalitarianism: everyone is treated alike.
- What is said is more important than who says it.
- There is little small talk or preamble; a cup of coffee and then start.
- Communication style is friendly, polite, but very frank.
- Importance is attached to accuracy.
- Disagreement is expressed politely, but openly.

- Charisma is suspect.
- Claims are generally modest.
- Realism: worst scenarios get as much attention as best scenarios.
- "What happens if . . . ?" is a frequent question.
- Some pessimism is allowed; consideration is given to economic downturns.
- Wasting time is to be avoided whenever possible.
- Both sides try to appear reasonable and moderate.
- It is bad form to persuade or try the hard sell.
- Parties do not interrupt each other when speaking.
- Humorous cynicism is accepted.
- The pace is steady and consistent, but not overly hurried.
- The day should finish with items on the agenda agreed upon.
- Mutual agreements should be adhered to and relied upon.
- Payments are to be prompt.
- Protocol (meals, etc.) is given minimum importance.

The key to negotiating successfully with Finns is to be modest, low key, get to the point, and never depart from common sense. In a world of contentious globalization, international conflicts of interest, recurring paradoxes, and growing complexities of issues, a typical Finnish business meeting is a relatively straightforward, refreshing experience.

- Be frank, open, direct. Get to the point.
- Be modest and low key. Don't talk too fast, raise your voice, or gush.
- Use first names, dress casually, and be relaxed about protocol and hierarchy. Eat lunch quickly.
- Use understatement and humor.
- Go to the sauna and drink together if you can.
- Learn a few words of Finnish, read some of their history,

show that you are at least somewhat knowledgeable. Show that you know Finland is high tech and Western.

- Show interest in Finnish arts and sports.
- Pay attention to women; never underestimate the Finnish female.
- Give Finns physical and mental space. Let them get on with the job and don't hover or follow them around.
- Show you rely on them.
- Be punctual, finish action chains; Finns hate slovenliness and loose ends.
- Be just, keep your word, and don't let them down, ever.
- Pay debts quickly.
- Listen carefully to what Finns say—it's not much, but they really mean it.
- Share your planning with them early on and constantly ask for their ideas. If you don't, they will proceed alone to an entrenched position from which it will be difficult to dislodge them.
- Be faithful and solid. Send Christmas cards.
- Remember, in Finnish eyes a statement is often regarded as a promise.
- Enjoy shared silences. In Finland silence is cozy, restful—even fun.
- Don't praise the Swedes or Russians too much.

LADIES AND GENTLEMEN

In previous chapters of this book we have examined questions and problems that arise when two or more cultures come into contact with each other—overlapping or clashing. So far, we have referred in the main to Finland's national cultural characteristics. Culture, in the sense that it represents one's outlook and worldview, is not, however, a strictly national phenomenon.

Regional, urban, corporate, and even family cultures can often be distinguished from national culture. But perhaps the greatest cultural divide is not national, religious, corporate, or ethnic, but sexual. Women, as Rex Harrison told us, are not like men. It is quite possible that an Italian woman has a world outlook more similar to that of a Finnish woman than to that of a male Italian.

We have discussed earlier the monochromatic traits of Germans, Swedes, Finns, and so forth, as well as the polychromatic ones of Italians, Brazilians, Arabs, etc. There is a cultural chasm between these two types in terms of their sense of time, use of space, and organizational priorities. Yet women (in any culture) can multitask better than men. They may be patient, efficient, organized, punctual, and reliable, but men often see them as extroverted, talkative, inquisitive, whimsical, changeable, and emotional. The role of a woman in society, especially when she is a mother, implies ipso facto that she is people-oriented, works any hours, and does several things at once.

Finnish women, as I've mentioned earlier, are considerably more open and communicative than Finnish men. They are, in fact, quite remarkable and deserve their own chapter.

Finnish Women

Cultural traits attributed to Finns in earlier chapters, particularly with regard to communication, reflect attitudes of the Finnish *male* in social and business situations. Finnish women, while sharing many of the same characteristics, are nevertheless much more out-going and approachable than the men, displaying few signs of uneasiness in the presence of foreigners. The Finnish woman could be described as strong-willed, adventurous, restless, often fearless, not without charm, and decidedly in love with life. Her level of edu-cation is second to no one in the world of women, and this gives her a feeling of self-confidence, which, allied with her sense of adven-ture and natural sisu, makes her, increasingly, a force to be reckoned with in the area of business.

As a communicator, she outshines her male counterpart. She often commands three or four languages, and at a two-day inter-national seminar for secretaries that I spoke at recently, I noticed that the Finnish delegates spoke better English than any other nationality, including the six British girls attending! Finnish women, unlike their men, play their full part in a two-way conversation, not missing their "turn" and shunning the reflective silences so popular with Finnish males. They combine charm with efficiency when presenting, use feminine intuition when negotiating, and generally think multidimensionally rather than in a linear fashion. The Finnish woman has many of the communicative qualities that the Finnish male would dearly like to have. With foreigners she does not always find the right message, but she usually finds the right *response.*

Her position in Finnish society and business, though not en-tirely what she would wish it to be, is superior to that of women in most other cultures: African and Arab women play virtually no part in business. In Japan, Latin America, Southeast Asia, and the Mediterranean countries, they are excluded from higher levels of industry and commerce. American women, while active in business, often fail to gain access to crucial power networks within their own companies and often lose their jobs if they move from city to city as their husbands are transferred in the typically mobile American business environment. Even in France, Germany, and Britain, where women play active roles, women find it hard to regain their position when their careers are interrupted by childbearing and mothering.

There have been and are some outstanding examples of female top executives in Europe—Pilar Miró, head of Spanish television; Ellen Schneider-Lenne, Deutsche Bank board director; Vasso Papandreo, European commissioner of social affairs; Birgit Breuel, chief executive of the Vorstand Treuhandanstalt; the legendary parfumier Paloma Picasso. In politics, Maggie Thatcher, Melina Mercouri, France's controversial former prime minister Edith Cresson, and Iceland's woman president Vigdis Finnbogadottir are household names. Norway could make a good case for being Europe's most developed land of equal opportunities for women—Prime Minister Gro Harlem Brundtland had seven women in her cabinet, and half the police force are women, too! It is, however, a cold fact that of all top business executives in the EU only 3 percent are women. (In the U.S. the corresponding figure is 2 percent, and in Japan it does not reach 1 percent!)

Finnish women were given the vote early, have long been experienced in political and commercial fields, and are probably destined to assume important functions in an integrating European environment. Certainly they are less afraid of foreign men than male Finns are of foreign women, and the numerous mixed marriages involving Finns usually feature the Finn as the female partner. Outstanding Finnish women in business and politics have included Tarja Halonen, president of Finland; Anneli Jäätteenmäki, prime minister; Elisabeth Rehn, minister of defense; Riitta Uosukainen, speaker of Parliament;

Sirkka Hämäläinen, governor, Bank of Finland; Annikki Saarela, board member, Postipankki; Sari Baldauf, Nokia, president, Cellular Systems; Pirkko Alitalo, board member for Pohjola; Raili Nuortila, managing director, Chemical Industry Federation; Reetta Meriläinen, editor-in-chief, *Helsingin Sanomat;* Pirkko Työläjärvi, governor, Turku and Pori County; and Eva-Riitta Siitonen, governor, Uusimaa County.

Even former Finnish beauty queens, such as Marja-Liisa Ståhlberg, Pirkko Mannola, and Lenita Airisto impress audiences with their linguistic abilities, level of education, and business acumen. The following statistics indicate that Finnish women are steadily consolidating their influential position in Finnish government and society:

Parliament	Out of 200 MPs, 74 are women
Government	Out of 18 ministers, 8 are women
Secondary school graduates 2002	Boys 14,874; Girls 21,321
Students in all universities 2002	Boys 79,900; Girls 90,100

The trend for the future is quite clear. Given her outgoing nature and ability to establish early rapport with non-Finns, the Finnish woman is probably under-utilized in international intercourse. Bypassing the shyness, modesty, and taciturnity of the Finnish male, she has much of the attractive, human-oriented magnetism that is required in a negotiator, presenter, manager of a foreign subsidiary, or even ambassador. While she firmly retains a healthy sense of her own ethnic identity, her exploratory leanings have encouraged her to develop the psychological skills needed to reduce the tensions that lead to conflict and to enable her to participate successfully in ethnic cultures differing widely from her own.

At the time of writing, the difference in levels of articulation between Finnish men and women are still readily apparent, especially in front of foreigners. The gap is, however, narrowing, for Finnish male executives, with their rapidly increasing English language skills, are learning to relate to at least Anglo-Saxons and Northern Europeans with diminished reticence. It is only a question of time before they have sufficient contact with Latins, Arabs, and other more distant peoples to develop confidence in addressing them with more vigor and verve. Also, Finnish women, though talkative and immensely curious about everything, themselves admit that in their innermost being they share the national shyness.

Finally, many a Finnish male executive has conceded that his effectiveness is due in no small part to the capable, well-educated, and talented secretary or personal assistant (PA) positioned behind him. In many cases she is low profile, even invisible, but her role is probably more important than in most countries. The next step to executive status is a small one for the Finnish high-level secretary, but a daunting one for many other nationals. Although the Finnish business world is still a man's world at this writing, things are changing. How will male Finnish managers cope in the future if this army of female PAs emerges from behind the curtain? What a potential to be realized!

Feminism in Finland

The world recognizes the strong position of women in the United States; their social status, influence, articulateness in public affairs, and high profile in political life are undeniable. Such is the structure of the Nordic societies, however, that women seem to enjoy some built-in advantages that women in the United States and many European countries have failed to acquire. Ms. Kari Mattila, former president of Union, a Finnish women's suffragette organization, comments that although women in Finland felt that feminism came from the U.S., they were in fact in a more advanced position in the Nordic area. Finnish women were given the vote in 1906 (only New Zealand had enfranchised women earlier, in 1893). American women did not get the vote until 1920, French women waited until 1944, and the Swiss were finally granted this honor in 1971! Apart from the question of political power, though, the women's vote seems to bear little relation to their social position in other respects. In France, to give one example, women have always enjoyed high status not only in the family but also socially and culturally. In Switzerland women played an important part in the development of the country's economy, and the Swiss were the first to extend university education to women on a basis of complete equality with men.

The voting system in Finland, which enables voters to choose from a large number of candidates, favors, in Mattila's opinion, the election of more women, who would be less inclined and equipped to face the hurly-burly of the head-to-head political fighting that is more common in other countries. Nearly half of Nordic ministers are women, who also hold important civil service positions. The first priority of the Finnish feminist is to earn her own living and have children, too. Finnish women see these two activities as contemporaneous events.

In the United States, by contrast, a graph showing the employment rates of women by age group typically consists of a two-humped curve, one high peak at the ages of 18–20, then a steep decline until roughly the age of 35, after which there is a second, lower and flatter peak (whose level in recent years has been progressively rising) for the age group 35–55.

In Finland the picture is somewhat different. The national welfare system allows women to go back to work early after childbearing. Fathers, who are granted paternity leave, often stay at home and do the housework. Even more important is the ubiquitous provision of communal child-care, enabling Finns to place their offspring in the care of skilled daycare providers during working hours. They see American women as underprivileged in this regard, with so many driving chores that they cannot hold down a full-time job. Many Finnish women do not bother to get married in the early years of a relationship; they see American women in an uncomfortable cycle of marry, divorce, marry again imbroglio—not conducive to cementing one's social or professional status.

The question of professional qualification and status has been mentioned by the former head of the Finnish Secretaries' Association, Ms. Pirkko Tuomisto, now an honorary member of the European Association of Professional Secretaries. Tuomisto, who at one time was Finland's most famous PA in her role as assistant to the chairman of Neste Oy, the Finnish oil company (then number one in the country in assets and often profits), sees a sizeable gap in the level of education of Finnish and Scandinavian secretaries on the one hand and American and some Europeans on the other. Finnish secretaries often work in a very independent manner and know much more about, for instance, the United States than American secretaries know about Europe. She considers that her American counterparts are in some respects blinkered, lacking in international awareness, and not evincing any particular interest in that area. Finnish businesswomen possess a voracious appetite for internationalism. She notes that Finnish (male) bosses are second to none in allowing their assistants to attend international conferences and conventions.

Both Mattila and Tuomisto agree that feminism in Finland is currently at an extremely low point. The peak was 1970–1975. Real feminists criticized the three-thousand-year-old patriarchal system, which has been clearly rebuffed in Nordic countries. In the new situation, women tend to be organized more in the form of work groups and concentrate on specific issues. Prominent Finnish women are firmly integrated in the political, administrative, and social systems, though they still highly value home and husband.

Unfortunately, though, in the Nordic nations as well as in the United States and much of Europe, women still face psychological and practical problems. In Finland the dual task of career and home brings, more often than not, serious overloading, even for women imbued with sisu.

CHAPTER
THIRTEEN

CONCEPTS OF SPACE AND TIME

Finnish concepts of space and time vary considerably from those of Americans and other Europeans; they merit close attention when we study Finnish psychology.

Space

A Finn requires a lot of space, both physically and mentally. Five million Finns live in an area measuring 337,000 square kilometers, which means that each square kilometer is inhabited by an average of 15 people, say four or five families, most of them on the quiet side. The Finnish love of elbowroom is similar to that of the American. (The population density of the United States is no more than 27 persons per square kilometer.) Finns revel in the size of their country (fifth largest in Europe, except for Russia) and cherish the concept of virtually empty land stretching out as far as they can see. The most famous and popular view in Finland is that seen from the rocky heights of Koli, where a labyrinth of forests, lakes, rivers, and outcrops of granite unfolds silently toward a distant horizon.

Finnish houses are as roomy as their inhabitants can afford to

151

make them, though the cost of heating imposes some restrictions. Rooms tend to be light and airy, and a succession of well-known Finnish architects have created homes and public buildings notable for the maximization of space and light. Alvar Aalto's Finlandia Talo is a good example. Other structures such as the Parliament building and Saarinen's Railway Station impress one because of the massiveness of their exterior, as do many generously proportioned statues by Finnish sculptors. Modern Finnish conference centers and corporate training establishments are striking in their size and amplitude and are often located in the heart of the forest or by the lakeside.

Finnish love of size and space has an interesting corollary—hatred of crowded conditions or close physical contact. A Finn's "space bubble"—or personal territory—is a circle of 1.2 meter radius, and woe betide the Italian or Mexican who invades it! While Britons can just barely tolerate the proximity of Latins when on holiday, Finns feel ill at ease with anyone inside their bubble and barely succeed in concealing their irritation if the proximity persists. They will accept a hug or even a kiss (female) in a good-natured manner, as long as it is clear that it is just a one-off occasion.

I once asked a Finnish peasant how much personal space he felt he had a right to. He was a man who took such questions seriously, so he thought about it for a full minute. Then he took his *puukko* (woodman's knife) out of its sheath and stretched his right arm out in front of him, holding the puukko with the blade parallel to the ground. "That distance," he replied.

When forming a bus queue, the first Finn to arrive normally leaves a space of five to ten meters between him- or herself and the bus stop. Others stand in line behind the first at intervals of two meters. I took a photograph of such a queue some time ago and showed it to some Italian friends, who refused to believe it was a bus queue. They understood that the lady who was first might not want to speak to the man behind her, but was she afraid of the bus stop?

Once on the bus, Finns avoid each other like they might have the bubonic plague. No one sits together unless there are no more vacant seats. When this happens, they do not talk. I used to take a late bus from Helsinki to Haukilahti—normally there would be five or six passengers at that time of night. For years I never observed anyone sitting together except for couples and friends. One night as I climbed onto the bus, I saw two men sitting together, even though the rest of the bus was empty. They were obviously strangers, as they did not converse; the one in the window seat simply stared out of the window. Why were they sitting on the same double seat? I was so intrigued, I placed myself across the aisle and after a few minutes commented in Finnish on the weather to the other man, who had given me a brief smile. When I spoke, he smiled broadly, threw his arms up in the air and replied, *"Mi scusi, non parlo finlandese, sono italiano."*

When a Finn builds his country log cabin, his inclination, as I've mentioned earlier, is to erect it at the maximum possible distance from the nearest neighbor. If his cabin cannot be readily observed by others and he still has a view over the lake, he has been successful. One does not generally observe "neighborly love" in Finland like what one occasionally sees in the United States, Japan, and sometimes in suburban Britain. Newcomers to a district, even in cities, are not knocked over in the rush of friendly people from next-door wanting to know if they can be of help while settling in. Americans and Australians excel in these strategies for meeting and getting to know strangers.

Finns, in contrast, assume that newcomers wish to maintain privacy unless they send strong signals to the contrary. Country neighbors two or three miles apart may go their entire lives without speaking to each other. No malice is intended, though suspected encroachment on one's own "territory" by another would quickly lead to anger.

There is little doubt that the idea of solitude—quiet guaranteed privacy—is high on the list of Finnish delights. When neighbors do meet (and find that they are compatible), true friendships ensue and mutual help is generous. But that help is seldom requested ("thou shalt not be in debt to others").

Finnish love of solitude leads Finns to excel in solitary, lonely sports, where constant contact with team members is not required. They are the world's best rally drivers, even doing well in Formula One. In this century most of their world records in sporting events have been set in long-distance running, long-distance skiing, and ski jumping. Sailing in the archipelago is another way Finns escape the madding crowd; Harri Harkimo, the son of a friend of mine, sailed round the world, solo, twice. When skiing in Lapland and other lonely places, one frequently sees solitary skiers, unlike the groups more common in France, Italy, Austria, and the United States.

I commented earlier that you have to give Finns mental as well as physical space. They hate being crowded, in any sense. Opinions cannot be forced on them, neither do they like close instructions on how to do anything. They have a developed sense of their own individual capability and resent being monitored. At the workplace, Finnish managers are well aware of this. To get the best out of their staff, they plan an early meeting at which the tasks of the day are outlined. Markku, assigned a certain job, then goes away and does it. You may not see him again till four o'clock, particularly if the task is time-consuming. But when he reports in at the end of the day, the job is usually done, and well done at that. Well-meaning interference may well result in your being handed the task to do yourself. Pride in one's workmanship is paramount with the Finn.

One last comment on the Finnish concept of space and location: *Finns must have a base.* It may be the home, office, or a hut in the forest, but they need to anchor somewhere. Without a base or anchorage Finns become insecure and quickly irritable. We noticed this year after year when we organized summer courses for them in Britain. At Heathrow they were not happy until they were all in the bus. They handled the ride well, but once at the course center, where registration and room allocation often took half an hour or so, they were like cats on hot bricks. If you hovered around them during the settling-in period, they brought up complaint after complaint: the beds were too soft, the taps leaked, bulbs had burnt out, they had seen a moth. We soon learned to make ourselves scarce during the first hour after arrival. After that, they had solved all the problems in good Finnish style, hung up their crisp, clean shirts and dresses, hidden their duty-free bottles, and "set up base." When we joined them in the bar, they were as contented as the fabled Cheshire Cat.

Time

Each culture has a different concept of time. No two are identical. Time has fascinated humanity throughout history: how to measure it, how best to use it. One's attitude toward time can be described in various ways: linear, monochronic, polychronic, circular, and so on. *Monochronic* means that you do one thing at a time in a planned order. *Polychronic* implies that you prefer to attempt several tasks simultaneously, thereby gaining time or benefiting from certain linkages between activities. The *circular* concept of time is adhered to by several Asian cultures that see in the rotation of the seasons and heavenly bodies annual or periodic renewal of events, options, and opportunities.

The Finnish concept of time is almost exclusively monochronic. Good planners, they set out their immediate tasks in order of priority and begin solving them, pragmatically, one by one. Figure 13.1 illustrates this linearity.

Polychronic, or multi-active, cultures plan their use of time in a way Finns disapprove of. In countries like Italy or Brazil, people do many things simultaneously and, in Finnish eyes, often rather sloppily. Finnish single-mindedness dictates that one finishes one's task fully, completely, and well. Only then should one proceed to the next task. The Latin reply that one gets more accomplished in the same time period by doing several things at once makes Finns laugh. How can you concentrate on one thing while thinking about another? The Italians *can*, of course, but it is not in the Finnish mindset.

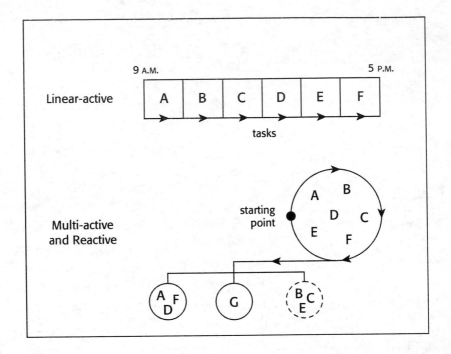

FIGURE 13.1   Concepts of Time

Polychronic people also interrupt each other (a cardinal sin in Finland) and carry on two or three conversations at the same time. A Finn attending a meeting where this happens is both confused and annoyed. Where is order? How can you listen to (and absorb) two conversations simultaneously? Again, Latins *can*. Nordics, especially Finns, cannot. French or South American long-windedness seems a terrible waste of time to Finns (who are often defenseless, as their culture doesn't allow them to interrupt). If these remarks make the Finns sound like testy, easily irritated individuals, they are only occasionally so because Finnish culture sets a high premium on conciseness, clarity, and economical use of time. Brits, other Nordics, U.S. Americans, and some Germans would agree with them. As far as bus queues or lines in post offices are concerned, the Finnish attitude is like the British: first come, first served. Anyone taking another's turn or place, even with a good excuse, will earn contempt.

When contemplating past, present, and future time, Finns—citizens of a young independent country—reveal relatively little past orientation when making plans (except where national security is involved: they remember the lessons they learned in the wars). Finns, highly technological and globalized, see the present as important, but as a present that will spawn rapid advances into the future. In this sense they are among the most future-oriented of peoples (along with the Americans). Of primary concern for the Finns, however, is the *immediate* future, for that is the frame in which they will realize their immediate goals and show proof of their efficient preparation for them.

Finns are known for their punctuality—they are the equal of the Germans in this regard. Germans are often accused of being time fanatics; the Swiss are said to suffer from a similar obsession. Finnish punctuality is less of an obsession than it is a reluctance to steal anyone else's time. At all events, Finns turn up on time for appointments and expect others to do so (if they are to be treated seriously). Like other Nordics, Finns like to make an early start in the morning and seem to experience no difficulty in getting up. Because of the restricted hours of daylight in winter, they are quite used to going to work in pitch blackness.

Other aspects of Finnish time keeping are taken for granted. Trains, buses, and airplanes generally leave and arrive on time. Finnish bus drivers make unscheduled stops in remote areas to pick up people but drive so skillfully in bad conditions that they are rarely late arriving at their destination. Appointment times are observed in business, and one is seldom kept waiting outside an executive's office. If you turn up late, you should have a reasonable excuse, one that will be accepted (once). Finns are not hurried during appointments, and you won't feel that "time is money" when dealing with them. They do, however, dislike obvious wastage of time and are irritated by verbosity or over-explicitness. They make allowance for Italians and other Latins.

Though Finns start work early, they also like to leave early, as

I've mentioned previously; they value their leisure time. Moments spent outdoors are valuable to them, and at certain times of the year they wish to maximize their exposure to what sunshine the North provides.

Finnish meals and mealtimes are a bit unusual. Because of the early start, few Finns indulge in a large breakfast. It may be only coffee, perhaps with toast. At work before eight, they are starving by 11:30, so this is when they take their lunch. Thirty to forty minutes is considered sufficient time for eating. The organization's canteen is usually available to provide rapid, efficient service and, more often than not, quite good food.

Protocol at the table is not an issue. Even visitors are expected to eat quickly and informally, and if meetings involve other Nordics, sandwiches offered as a meeting progresses may suffice, particularly if the visitors intend to return to Stockholm or Oslo the same day. When French hosts take them out for three-hour lunches, Finns often wonder if the French take business seriously. The French, treated to lightning-fast Finnish business lunches, often wonder the same thing! Business dinners in Finland held for visiting foreigners are often more elaborate, with considerable amounts of alcohol being offered. These dinners are still quite early for Latin tastes (6:30 or 7:00 P.M.).

Most Finnish families eat at home as early as 5:00 or 5:30. The resultant long evenings are obviously for outdoor activity or, in winter, reading, the cinema, and theater. Finns are well versed in the arts and devote a lot of their time to artistic pursuits. A word of warning: cocktail parties or drinks after dinner can be prolonged indefinitely by Finnish guests if you adhere to the practice of displaying an unlimited amount of liquor (on a drink-or-return arrangement with the caterers). Finns do not like to leave behind bottles that are full or even half-full.

One interesting aspect of the Finnish concept of time strikes a parallel with that of the Japanese. This is a close association of certain activities with specific times of the year. As in Japan, the year unfolds in a traditional manner. Finns show close adherence to the implications of their climate and seasons. Midsummer is the best example of this—it is the most cherished ritual—but Christmas and the various *pikku-joulut* (little Christmases) are not far behind. The sauna is a weekly ritual, picking various berries and mushrooms is a seasonal one. Helsinki *empties* in summer, for this is the time when families pack themselves off to the country—the ritual of the lakeside cabin or summerhouse. Father goes for at least a month, or every evening if it is within driving distance of his workplace. Other rituals that are strictly observed are student graduations, the Finland-Sweden track meet, and of course the precious skiing holiday.

Finns take care of their possessions in a timely manner. The leaking tap, the faulty oven, the plugged drain do not go long without being repaired. Whether it is the house, boat, wristwatch, or his teeth, the Finn likes everything in pristine condition. Carpenters and plumbers are in great demand—often difficult to persuade to come—but most Finns readily pay money under the table to secure quick service.

Finns also like to be well stocked up—food, liquor, winter logs, clothes—they are seldom caught without. They buy well in advance, regarding it as part of good planning.

To close, allow me to share a final story about the Finnish attitude toward time when traveling. It is an eye-opener to take the evening boat from either Helsinki or Turku to Stockholm. I have done this many times, and in the old days the ships were relatively small. Arrival in Stockholm used to be scheduled for 7:00 in the morning. If you were still in bed at 6:00, you would notice that the boat had started to list to port. If, alarmed, you went on deck, you would see several hundred Finns standing guard over rows of luggage, by the port rail. For as long as an hour they would stand there, bleak, resolute, braving the cold and sometimes fleeting snow, like a silent army waiting to go into battle. Things have changed a little with the new liners, but most of the interior passageways are still clogged with spotless suitcases and their spotless owners well before Stockholm's elegant spires rise above the horizon. The motto of the international Boy Scouts' movement, "Be Prepared," describes Finns perfectly.

HUMOR

Finnish humor shares many of the characteristics of Scandinavian humor, inasmuch as it can be beautifully dry and pithy, but, surprisingly, it is more varied than straight Scandinavian humor, perhaps on account of the various influences that the Finns have been subject to from East and West.

Many people on a short visit to Finland may leave with the impression that humor plays little part in Finnish life. Finns do not open up on the first few days of contact with strangers, and their guarded, serious faces show little of the lively activity going on behind the "mask."

The theatrical expressions and gestures of many French or Spanish people easily lead you to believe that these persons are capable of great humor. Englishmen often have humorous wrinkles around the eyes, and their occasional eccentricities reinforce the feeling that they could be very funny. Rural Australians, severely wrinkled by the sun, frequently bear a humorous appearance (a bunch of Crocodile Dundees, we might think) and, indeed, Australians almost rival the Americans in their tendency to wisecrack. Greek, Sicilian, and other Mediterranean people often have humorous curves around the mouth, lips, and chin.

The Finn, however, has been taught from birth not to screw up his face in an exaggerated manner to demonstrate to others what his feelings are. If a Frenchman says *"Je ne sais pas,"* he throws both arms out as if he is being crucified and shrugs his shoulders in a manner risking dislocation. A Spaniard evincing anger often appears apoplectic. The Finn shies away from such behaviour. The rules permit him to smile and show mild surprise or hope, but disappointment, disgust, anger, and euphoria are feelings to be concealed behind a straight face. A good Finn keeps his face in repose. A face in repose often bears a glum expression—fairly standard in Finnish offices, conferences, and on the street. If you visit in winter, you might say they have a lot to be glum about.

But you should not be misled into thinking the Finns are gloomy and humorless. On the contrary, they are very interested in humor, they experiment with humor, they are, in fact, hungry for humor. Humor, as I have mentioned earlier, thrives on incongruity and paradox. Facing incongruity, recognizing and dealing with it, seeing it in perspective, is excellent training in the field of humor. Young, culture-rich, war-battered, prosperous, pessimistic Finland, still sorting out the paradoxes attendant on the process of an ancient culture adapting with incredible speed to its transformation into an ultramodern state, is a showcase for (rather entertaining) incongruity.

Any people creating a successful society above 60°N latitude must be gifted with or quickly develop a keen sense of perspective. The severe climate has made the Finns a nation of sun-lovers—this is only natural—but other paradoxes are harder to explain and bear repeating here. Finns have achieved incredible feats, but insist that foreigners are cleverer than they are. They are brilliant linguists, but declare the opposite. They are sophisticated in art, technology, and social institutions, but insist they are rude and clumsy. They are warm-hearted people, but have a desire for solitude. They love freedom, but are experts in curtailing their own liberty.

These national contradictions show a complexity of character with a wide range of feelings. Such width facilitates a true sense of proportion—the relative importance of things. The hardships suffered by the Finnish people, the incongruous juxtaposition of their tiny nation and her mammoth neighbour, the driving will to survive, all these factors produce a special sense of humor.

Dryness

Dryness is an essential element of Finnish humor. Urho Kekkonen was Finland's president for twenty-six years, a cunning Finn who felt he saw things in proportion. He liked the good life as well as the hard world of politics—he probably manipulated Khruschev and Brezhnev in a way few others could. One evening it is said that Kekkonen indulged in hearty eating and drinking in the Kämp Restaurant in downtown Helsinki. It was rumored that the drinking led to brawling and fisticuffs involving the president. The next morning the Finnish newspapers—always discreet at that time—reported that "a well-known Finnish politician had been involved in a fight in a first-class restaurant." Kekkonen, who was the unnamed target of the article, issued a short statement denying any part in the affair, dryly adding that the Kämp was not a first-class restaurant.

Finnish dryness is evident in the following story about Kekkonen and Ahti Karjalainen, the not-so-clever foreign minister (Karjalainen jokes abound in Finland).

Urho Kekkonen dies and goes to heaven. St. Peter interviews him at the Pearly Gates. Name? Urho Kekkonen. Job? President of Finland. St. Peter takes out a thick file and studies it for a few minutes. Then he extracts one sheet and says, "Yes, here we are, entrance permitted. Let me give you the details of the program here. Wake-up call at seven o'clock, breakfast at eight, read newspaper from nine till ten. Then the morning walk around heaven with your girlfriend on your arm. Lunch is at . . ."

"Girlfriend?" interrupts Kekkonen anxiously. "Who is my girlfriend?" St. Peter consults what appears to be a list of couples.

"Let me see—Karjalainen, Kekkonen, Kennedy—here you are—your girlfriend is Golda Meir."

"Golda Meir!" shouts Kekkonen in disgust. "I don't want Golda Meir! Why her?"

"Well, you see," replies St. Peter, "it all depends on your record on earth. You probably know that as a politician you did not always uphold satisfactory moral standards. You deceived voters, you made false promises, you often lied. You may say that having Golda Meir as a girlfriend is a kind of punishment."

"That's enough!" shouts Kekkonen, "I will hear no more of this. I am leaving heaven!" And he walks out through the Pearly Gates.

Once outside, however, his curiosity gets the better of him and he walks around the perimeter of heaven until 10:00 A.M. Heaven is surrounded by a low wall and he can easily see over it. At ten o'clock all the couples come out for their morning walk. Kekkonen recognizes famous people such as Shakespeare and Sibelius with attractive companions. Suddenly, he sees Ahti Karjalainen with Marilyn Monroe on his arm. Kekkonen is furious. He rushes back to the entrance of heaven and angrily addresses St. Peter.

"I know that I was not exactly a saint when I was on earth, but Ahti Karjalainen was not much better. He made false promises, he lied as often as I did, and, moreover, he was stupid! And you give him Marilyn Monroe as a girlfriend!"

"No, you have to look at it another way," replies St. Peter, "You see, Ahti Karjalainen is Marilyn Monroe's punishment."

Taciturnity

Traditional Finnish jokes love to nurture the Finn stereotype—the strong-willed, taciturn, hard-drinking individual who has the cool head to cut through undue fuss, theatrical behavior, and exaggeration. Marshal Mannerheim, the Finnish guest of honor at a seventeen-course dinner given by a gushing Swedish hostess, found her waiting at the door expecting lavish compliments from the guests as they left. "Thank you, madam, the bread was excellent," said Mannerheim as he passed through the doorway.

Such stories about the marshal are legion. His barman, whenever he broke a glass, would salute stiffly in front of Mannerheim and ask to be transferred to the Russian front. When a German general asked Mannerheim's aide at a joint military briefing if he could smoke a cigar in the marshal's presence, the reply was, "I don't know. Nobody ever tried it before."

Finnish stories about national taciturnity are endless. A favorite is about the two Finns who drink a dozen cognacs as they watch the midnight sun hover around the horizon, all without saying a word. Finally, Paavo grunts, "Nice sky. . . ."

"Have we come here to drink or chatter all the time?" shouts Juhani.

The following anecdote, which deals with the taciturnity of the people living in the provinces of Häme and Pohjanmaa in central Finland, arouses different responses according to the culture of the reader:

One day a horse and cart from Häme meet a horse and cart from Pohjanmaa on the bridge leading from one province to the other. The Häme driver, who is on the bridge first, finds his cart blocked by that from Pohjanmaa. The bridge is too narrow for the carts to pass each other and neither driver wishes to converse with the other.

The Häme cart driver takes out his newspaper and begins to read. Nobody speaks and he reads on for half an hour.

After thirty minutes, the Pohjanmaa driver gets down from his cart, walks over to the other, and taps the Häme reader on the knuckles.

"When you have finished reading it, I'll have it for an hour."

The Italians find this story funny inasmuch as it illustrates how incredibly phlegmatic Nordics can appear in Italian eyes. They see the joke as denigrating the Finns, toward whom they feel a sense of superiority. Brits find the story funny because it reminds them of Yorkshiremen. Germans consider it to have merit but are uneasy about the time lost. Finns find it funny because it confirms a stereotype that they love to believe in, but, unlike the Italians, they do not see the story as one that denigrates their way of life. On the contrary, it emphasizes Finnish calmness, unflappability, and patience.

Another story in the same vein:

Virtanen, wandering around Greece, came across a monastery and was allowed in for a meal. He told the Abbot he would like to stay there, as he was tired of the modern world.

"You are very welcome," replied the Abbot. "We need more inmates here to till the fields and maintain the buildings. But I must tell you that we have certain rules. There are only two meals a day—porridge in the morning and soup in the evening. You must work ten hours a day, and we observe at all times the rule of silence. You are not allowed to speak at all."

"No problem for a Finn," said Virtanen, "in fact it will make a nice change after Helsinki."

Virtanen worked at the monastery for five years without speaking. At the end of this time he was summoned to the Abbot, who told him, "You have been an excellent worker. As a reward you are allowed to say two words."

"I'm hungry," replied Virtanen.

"Give Virtanen an extra bowl of soup this evening," said the Abbot to the cook.

Virtanen worked another five years in silence and once more was asked to see the Abbot. "Your fine work has continued," said the good man. "You are permitted to say two more words."

"I'm cold," said Virtanen.

"Give Virtanen an extra blanket from December to March,"
instructed the Abbot.

After a further five years, Virtanen was summoned again. "You
have performed magnificently once more," said the Abbot. "Your
reward is to speak two more words."

"I'm going," said Virtanen.

Visitors to Finland are quick to notice that Finnish women are
much more loquacious than the men. The taciturnity of the Finnish
male is often a source of frustration among the women—who are
perhaps yearning for a little romance from time to time.

Sirkka: "Markku! You never tell me that you love me."
Markku: "Listen, twenty-five years ago when we were about to get
married, I told you that I loved you. If there is any change in the
situation, I will let you know."

Finnish diplomats attending EU meetings in Brussels are already
acquiring a special reputation.

Recently, a vice minister leaving an important meeting was
besieged by the usual crowd:
    "What can you tell us, Mr. Vice Minister?"
    "No comment."
    "Nothing at all?"
    "That's right. And don't quote me!"

Ambassador Pertti Salolainen tells the story of the Finnish ambassador to Italy in 1939, who was asked to submit his annual
report on events there. Political activity at the time was particularly
feverish and controversial on account of Mussolini's relations with
Hitler. The report said, "Nothing has happened in Italy this year."
The Finnish Foreign Office telegraphed the ambassador, asking him

to be more explicit and submit a longer report. The amended version read, "Nothing has happened in Italy this year that is of interest to Finland."

> How can you tell a Finnish extrovert?
> He stares at *your* shoes.

Saarinen, the world-famous Finnish architect who created so many fine buildings in the United States, was one day being interviewed by an American radio company. He was so slow in answering the questions that the interviewer was afraid they would not get through them in the half hour allotted for the broadcast. He explained the problem and asked Saarinen if he would speak faster.

"No," said Saarinen.

"Then how shall we fit everything in?"

"I can always say less."

Toughness

Besides taciturnity, toughness is another Finnish trait that is emphasized in Finnish anecdotes:

During the Italian-Albanian war, the Italians encountered unusually stiff resistance in a particular battle zone, and their intelligence indicated that the Albanians were being helped by a Finnish force. After heavy losses one day, Rome sent a telegram to Helsinki asking the Finnish government to "withdraw the Finnish contingent."

After some investigation, Helsinki replied that the rumor about a Finnish contingent was a myth. The only Finns they could identify in Albania were two old soldiers, long retired: Sergeant Aalto and Private Leppänen.

"Those are the two we mean," said the next Italian telegram, *"Get them out!"*

A political analyst was doing a survey on the number of Russian troops still left in the Baltic states in the early 1990s. He felt he needed to know how many Russian military personnel (if any) were still in Finland. He phoned a colonel he knew and asked him if he could check on this for him.

"Certainly," the colonel replied, "just give me twenty minutes."

He rang back soon with the answer: "Four hundred thousand and four."

The political analyst was dumbfounded. "So many?" he asked.

"Yes, four of them are still alive."

Soininen, a tough Finnish lumberjack who was unemployed in Finland for some time, emigrated to the United States to seek work. He did not have much success until one day a company agreed to employ him on a trial basis.

"American lumberjacks are very fast," the manager told Soininen. "They cut down an average of 100 trees per day. You will have to be able to the same."

Soininen said he would do his best, but he only managed to cut down 64 trees for the day. "Not enough," said the manager, "but we'll give you one more day's trial to see if you improve."

The next day Soininen cut lumber from 7:00 A.M. to 7:00 P.M. but had a total of only 85 trees.

"Not good enough," said the manager.

"Please give me one final day's trial," asked Soininen.

The American agreed and Soininen commenced work the next day at 6:00 in the morning. At 7:00 in the evening he staggered, exhausted, into the manager's office. "How many today?" the manager asked.

"Ninety-one. I've failed."

The manager decided to have a look at his chain saw to see if it was in good condition. He pulled the pull-cord and it started properly—apparently there was nothing wrong with it.

"What's that funny noise?" asked Soininen.

Hard Drinking

Some Finnish jokes about toughness include references to their hard-drinking habits.

How do you make a Finnish fisherman's coffee?

First you put a 1-mark coin in the bottom of a cup. Then you pour in coffee until the coin disappears from view. After that you pour vodka until you can read the date on the coin. The coffee is now ready to drink.

One day Toivo went out on the ice to fish. It was 25°C below zero and there was a cold wind. Two of his friends were worried about him, so they took him some hot coffee in a flask.

They found him well wrapped up in a thick overcoat, warm boots, woolen scarf, and gloves, but the earflaps of his fur hat were turned up instead of down. His ears were white and frozen. "Toivo," they exclaimed, "don't you know that those flaps should be turned down to protect your ears?"

"Yes, I know," he replied, "but yesterday I had them turned down and I had a terrible accident."

"Really? What happened?"

"Somebody asked me if I wanted a drink and I didn't hear him."

Another Finnish joke about drinking indicates the Finns' sense of perspective about this favorite subject:

A large moose was accustomed to drinking the water of a secluded pond in the depths of the Finnish forest. On such occasions he would admire his fine head and huge antlers reflected in the pond.

Often he would throw back his head and exclaim, "Who is King of the Forest?"

The only reply he received was the wind rustling in the surrounding pines.

He would then continue, "I am the King of the Forest!"

One day, however, after he had gone through this routine, a deep voice behind him growled, "What did you say, Mr. Moose?"

He turned and saw a huge wolf with glistening fangs. "Well, one talks such rubbish when one has been drinking," replied the moose hastily.

Hard drinking acquired an aura of tenuous respectability in Finland just after the turn of the century when Jean Sibelius, the great composer, indulged in three- to five-day drinking sprees with a group of leading Finnish intellectuals, painters, and architects. These binges took place in the Hotel Kämp in downtown Helsinki.

In the middle of one of these sessions, which were regular and well publicized, one of Sibelius' assistants interrupted the proceedings to take him aside and remind him that he was due to conduct a symphony that very evening in Vyborg, near the Russian border. Sibelius rushed to the railway station, boarded the eastbound train, and arrived in Vyborg in time to keep his appointment. When he rejoined his drinking partners the next morning, they were all sitting in exactly the same positions they were in when he left. They had not attached any importance to his temporary absence except one of them asked why he had taken so long to go to the toilet.

Other Sources

Finnish peasants, though traditionally considered slow-witted, have, in my experience, exhibited astonishingly spontaneous wit.

Several years ago, when I was working on a Finnish farm, half a dozen of us had been working with chisels and two-handed saws, on logs that had somehow got frozen into the surface of a lake. During our chiseling the ice suddenly broke and one of the laborers, Tuominen, fell headfirst through the hole, fully dressed and holding a two-handed saw. Just when he resurfaced, spluttering and choking, Oksanen, another peasant, arrived with coffee for us. Seeing Tuominen trying to climb out of the hole in the ice, he said, "What's happening here?"

"It's obvious, you idiot," shouted Tuominen, "the under-sawers are coming up for their coffee break."

On another occasion, Tähtinen, an eighteen-year-old from a poor family living in a modest farm cottage, arrived for the winter logging without his gloves. The son of the estate owner asked him rather abruptly where his gloves were.

"Oh dear, I've left them in the music room, under my mortarboard on the grand piano," replied Tähtinen. (A riposte worthy of any Frenchman, I thought.)

Karelian Finns have their own sense of humor. Two examples of this follow:

At the end of the war, over four hundred thousand Karelian Finns were resettled in Finland. Very few wished to remain in the Soviet Union. In some cases, however, farms were located right on the border, even split between the two countries. One Vepsäläinen, who had fifty fine hectares, was given the choice of declaring his farm Finnish or Russian. It was good land and authorities on both sides wanted to recruit him. They visited him and tried to persuade him. The Russian came first: "If you stay in Russia, your farm will be collectivized and you will not need to do all the work yourself. You will have many willing colleagues to help you if you are sick. And you will always have a market for your produce, as the state will buy it."

"I'll think about it," said Vepsäläinen. "Come back in three days."

Then he was visited by the local Finnish authorities, who told him, "Don't be too sure that collectivization is good for you. You won't own anything outright any more. Think of the freedom of action and decision that being in Finland will give you."

"I'll think about it," replied Vepsäläinen. "Come back in two days."

The two delegations came back two days later to hear his decision.

"I've decided to keep my farm in Finland," announced Vepsäläinen.

The Soviets, very disappointed, asked him why he had chosen thus.

"Well, I don't think I could stand the long Russian winter," replied Vepsäläinen.

Three Karelians, resettled in Finland, sit in a bar in Lahti. They are comparing hardship. "It was bad for me," says the first. "I was a crop farmer and I lost fifty hectares of beautiful arable land."

"It was worse for me," says the second. "I had woodland and I lost one hundred hectares of fine forest."

"It was even worse for me," says the third. "I lost the whole province!"

"What do you mean?" asked the first two.

"I was a tramp."

THE WILY WEASEL—
THE NOKIA STORY

In 1865 a twenty-five-year-old Finnish mining engineer named Fredrik Idestam founded a small forest products company in the Finnish inland town of Tampere. A few years later he moved his plant ten miles to the west along the River Nokia and called his enterprise Nokia Ab, after the river. The word *nokia* in Finnish means "weasel"—a somewhat less-than-inspiring name in translation, but two other companies founded in subsequent years—the Finnish Rubber Works in 1898 and the Finnish Cable Works in 1912—found it good enough to throw their lot in with Nokia (the formal merger being executed under the name Oy Nokia Ab in 1966). See Table 15.1 for a complete chronology.

The group did not have an auspicious beginning. The Rubber Works—the strongest of the three companies—lost money every year from 1898 to 1914, and the chief executive and primary owner, Eduard Polón, was exiled to Russia in 1916 and again in 1917. The three separate industries had little synergy. Both the wood products and rubber divisions needed large amounts of capital investment and faced stiff competition internationally.

Both divisions were ultimately divested as the group turned to focus on electronics. A large number of acquisitions in consumer

TABLE 15.1   The Nokia Chronology

1865	Nokia Ab founded; forest industry and power production
1898	Finnish Rubber Works (Suomen Gummitehdas Oy) established
1912	Finnish Cable Works (Suomen Kaapelitehdas Oy) established
1903–1906	Marshal C. G. Mannerheim was member of Nokia board
1900–1914	Relatively unrestricted world trade enabled Nokia to enter international markets
1914–1918	Finland stayed out of World War I. Nokia supplied Russia with war materiel. Eduard Polón amassed wealth to pave the way for establishment of the Nokia Group
1945–1952	Nokia heavily involved in manufacturing products demanded by Russians as war reparations
1952	After war reparations ended, Nokia continued to export vigorously to the Russian market. One-quarter of all cable sales went to the Soviets, who paid in oil
1960	Nokia entered the computer business
1967	Oy Nokia Ab Group established
1971	Nokia electronics made the first home-grown computer, the Mikko
1970s	Nokia commenced production of digital telephone exchanges in cooperation with Siemens and Ericsson
1983	Nokia acquired majority holdings in Salora and Luxor and entered the TV market
1987	Nokia made a large number of significant acquisitions. The company became badly over-stretched
1988	December Nokia CEO Kari Kairamo committed suicide

1988–1992	Simo Vuorilehto became president of Nokia. Difficult years involving downsizing
1989	Radiolinja placed first big order with Nokia—a digital GSM network
1991	Collapse of Soviet Union hit Nokia trade badly; large numbers of personnel in telecommunications were transferred to Mobile Phones
1992	Nokia handed over to Jorma Ollila
1994	Sales of mobile phones began to take off with 1994 showing an increase of 119 percent and 1995 an increase of 92 percent
	Nokia shares were listed on the NYSE
	Nokia switched the company language from Finnish to English.
	Nokia House was built as new headquarters
1995	Nokia Mobile Phones expanded its production facilities at its Bochum plant in Germany
1995–1996	Nokia divested itself of its traditional industries, selling cables, cable machinery, tires, industrial electronics, and consumer electronics
1996	Nokia's market value was estimated at equaling that of the combined value of Finland's forest and metal engineering industries as well as all banks and insurance companies
1998–2000	Nokia share price increases resulted in creation of many "Nokia Millionaires"
1998	World leadership achieved in the mobile phone industry
2000	Nokia employed 59,000 people
2001	Nokia had 1,500,000 U.S. shareholders
2001	Nokia employed 18,600 personnel in Research and Development at 54 centers in 14 different countries

electronics led to Nokia becoming one of Europe's top three television manufacturers. It was a disastrous move, producing eventual cumulative losses of more than one billion dollars. In December 1988 Nokia's chairman and chief executive, Kari Kairamo, committed suicide.

In the following decade Nokia's group operating profit went from €144 million (1990) to €5.8 billion in 2000. The market value of all Nokia stocks at year's end 1990 was €677 million. At year's end 2000 the total value stood at €222 billion. At this point Nokia was *Europe's largest company* by market capitalization. With the sale of 130 million mobile phones in 2000 the company had also achieved a unique position for a Finnish enterprise—that of world leader in a major industry.

The meteoric rise of Nokia in the last decade of the twentieth century is an astonishing, arguably unique commercial phenomenon, even in a period of history marked by startling political, scientific, and evolutionary change and advancement. Such an apparently miraculous transformation of a small company's fortunes therefore merits close attention. How was it achieved? What was the key?

A simple answer, in laconic Finnish parlance, would be that Nokia stumbled across the right product (the mobile phone) in the right place (Finland) at the right time (the IT Revolution). This is, in essence, not untrue, but what is difficult to comprehend is the very magnitude of the miracle, whereby a relatively small firm known for three-quarters of a century for producing rubber boots, tires, cables, and forest products suddenly announced it was the continent's biggest enterprise by market value, by virtue of its leading product, which it did not begin to manufacture before 1990!

There is no single key to Nokia's success. The factors are numerous and varied, but they can be grouped into three categories:

1. External factors
2. Internal management
3. The "Home Turf" Factor

External Factors

Although sound management must be given the chief credit for Nokia's spectacular success, a variety of external factors and circumstances proved fortunate for the company as well. For hundreds of years, and especially from 1809–1917, Finland lived in the shadow of her giant neighbor, Russia, with whom she shared a one-thousand-kilometer border and an uneasy political union.

The Russian Connection

Russian (and even Soviet) proximity, however, has not always been disadvantageous. Finland has, on several occasions in her history, "played the Russian card," both in her international dealings and in business. Relations with tsarist Russia, especially during the reign of Alexander III, were very good, and in the rather unrestricted period of world trade that continued up to 1914 the very size of the eastern neighbor's market was a tempting factor for Finnish firms.

Nokia was a clear beneficiary at this time, and especially from 1914 to 1917, when Russia was struggling to meet the needs of her war economy. The Russian military relied on Finnish industry for a lot of her war materiel. (It must be remembered that Finland still had the status of an autonomous Grand Duchy within the Russian Empire.) Eduard Polón, in spite of being exiled to Russia for his political opposition, was able to amass great wealth in this period, and this enabled him to lay the foundation for Nokia's expansion. The nature of the war alignment had reduced foreign competition for the Rubber Works, and the subsequent inflation wiped out most of the company's debts.

The Bolshevik Revolution in 1917 put an end to this situation. Finland had been directing virtually all her exports to Russia; shortly afterward, the establishment of an independent Finnish Republic led to a commercial volte-face, where Finnish firms (led by Nokia) turned their attention to Western Europe in the search for new markets.

Between the two world wars, Nokia's fortunes rose and fell in tandem with the slower-developing Finnish economy. World War II once again demonstrated the two-edged nature of the Russo-Finnish relationship. The Winter War of 1939–1940 and resumption of hostilities from 1940 to 1944 was bad news for Finland and her war-battered economy.

The imposition of war reparations to the Soviets ($300 million) was more bad news. Good news, however, followed not far behind for Nokia. As all reparations had to be made in specified industrial products, Nokia was involved up to the hilt. There was not much profit to be had, but when the cable quota of the reparations had been fulfilled in 1948 (cable products had amounted to nearly 6 percent of the total reparations), Nokia discovered that their Russian market was firmly established and were able to continue exports of power and relay cables, as well as cable machinery, through the 1950s and 1960s at a highly profitable rate.

Such external factors have proven very valuable to Nokia. The continuance of exports to a huge centralized economy like the Soviet Union not only brought in sizeable profits, paid for reliably and often in oil, but also gave Nokia executives valuable experience in dealing with a multilayered bureaucracy. Frustrations were many, but the Soviets ordered long lines of products and (until 1991) were quite predictable in their order volumes. Finnish executives, not only at Nokia, have frequently indicated that "they know how to deal with the Russians," and while this is true only up to a point, it is guaranteed to gain brownie points with many Western and particularly American colleagues and partners. The deft balancing act that Finland performs between East and West has more than once benefited the country (and Nokia) and is likely to continue to do so in the present volatile global shifting and the enigmatic, labyrinthine development of the new entrepreneurial Russia.

The 1950s and 1960s were profitable for Nokia's Russian business. In the early 1970s the news was even better. The oil price hikes of those years enabled the Soviet Union to double its imports from

Finland. When the oil price rose, so did the value of Nokia's exports. In 1977 Nokia exported products worth $120 million to the Soviets (mainly cable machinery).

Of particular interest to students of the Nokia success story is that in the 1960s and 1970s, partly due to the vigorous exports of the cable division, Nokia's electronic exports to the Soviet Union got under way. Initial exports in this field were multichannel analyzers, pulse code modulation for telephone networks, an electronic scoreboard for the Lenin Stadium in Moscow, and (watch it!) mobile phones.

However, the most significant electronics export to Moscow was the DX200 telephone exchange in the 1980s. This paved the way for Nokia to win complete communications systems in the West when the markets became deregulated late in the 1980s. Without the important contracts gained in the Soviet Union, Nokia might well have discontinued its production of telephone exchanges. It was a relatively new area for the company. If they had not received the initial encouragement from the Soviets, they might have left the way open for vigorous rivals such as Ericsson, Siemens, and U.S. firms.

Another external factor working in Nokia's favor was that in 1981 Finland's license administration refused to grant the Finnish subsidiary of LM Ericsson of Sweden an export license for the sale of products to the Soviet Union. This was not the only occasion when the Finnish state lent clear support to Nokia (a subject that we address later in this chapter under the "Home Turf" section).

In 1991 the Soviet Union collapsed; initially this hit Nokia hard. Sales to the East in January and February totaled less than half a million dollars as compared with $20 million planned in the budget. The Nokia management reacted with alacrity, cost cutting vigorously and concentrating on Western markets. Fortunately, another saving factor was at hand: a tremendous surge in cellular networks came just at the right time, enabling Nokia to transfer large numbers of personnel engaged in the lost Soviet fixed networks market to the mobile phone division.

Other Factors

Europe was changing fast. The Soviet collapse coincided with wide-ranging deregulation in several European countries, nowhere more so than in Finland itself. New telecom operators sprang up everywhere, and Nokia capitalized on the contacts it had been building in the Telecommunications division during the previous decade. Matti Alahuhta, head of Telecommunications, stressed the importance of entering these new markets early, maximizing the window of opportunity by concentrating on research and innovating boldly.

Nokia was continually a beneficiary of the willingness of the Finnish state to maximize deregulation in accordance with its democratic traditions. Deregulation in Finland occurred early and was consistent, forcing Nokia and other Finnish companies such as Kone and Valmet to seek rapid international expansion. In Nokia's case the breakthrough of digital mobile phones could hardly have been more timely. Finland—poor in raw materials—no longer needed to import costly copper and rubber. In the mobile phone industry only brainpower and research and development (R&D) were required.

Another external factor helping Nokia was a supply of cheap energy from Finland's new nuclear reactors. Also, the Finnish presidents succeeding the long-serving Urho Kekkonen, who had protected state-owned companies trading with the Soviet Union, adopted a more Western-oriented attitude. Finally, the withdrawal of the main Finnish banks from the domination of Nokia's financing and management and the Finnish government's removal of restrictions concerning foreign ownership of companies gave Nokia elbow room to diversify its shareholders, transforming a Finnish firm into a typically U.S. group and gaining access to almost unlimited international capital markets. Interestingly, rival Ericsson's shareholding (in Ericsson) is still 50 percent Swedish. Nokia's Finnish shareholders own 6 percent of Nokia.

Internal Management

Life can only be understood backward, but it must be lived forward. Seen in retrospect, many of the major decisions made by the Nokia management in the 1980s and 1990s are no less than visionary. It is true that the unfortunate foray into consumer electronics and the resulting losses led to a basically cautious management style and a bias toward organic growth, but subsequent judgments by Kairamo and Alahuhta and later by Ollila and Ala-Pietilä are typified by both boldness and prescience. It may well be that the most courageous decision of all was the divestiture of all the core industries upon which Nokia's reputation had been built (forest products, rubber, and cables). But the company's commitment to invest heavily and consistently in R&D has also proven decisive in enabling Nokia to stay ahead of the game and widen the technological gap between itself and competitors such as Ericsson and Motorola.

The Nokia Research Center was established as an information technology unit in 1979 with 50 employees. By 2001 Nokia employed 18,600 people. This involved about 35 percent of the company's workforce in R&D in 54 R&D centers in 14 countries. Sixty-three percent of Nokia's researchers are based in Finland. Nokia's research expenditure is substantially larger than public support it has received. In 1998 the company established the New Venture Fund with a capital of $100 million. This funded long-term research, often aimed at risky products. Innovation, not price, was seen as the key to profitability.

Another development group, called the Nokia Ventures Organization, was headed by the perspicacious Pekka Ala-Pietilä. This took on the form of a debating forum, gathering information about businesses not directly related to Nokia's existing operations, focusing instead on widening the company's horizons and keeping it alert to areas of future potential. Such alertness, combined with speed and agility in action, has become the hallmark of Nokia's style of operation. Flexibility and willingness to "reinvent" strategies have served Nokia well in an era of volatile demand and rapidly changing markets.

The visions and strategies of Nokia's leaders began to pay off, owing to the growth of mobile phones in the 1980s, which rapidly became a mass-market product. Nokia was an early adherent to the pan-Nordic Mobile Telephone System (NMT) that was introduced in 1981. A key element of this system was international mobility, paving the way for the coming Global System for Mobile Communications (GSM) system, which really took off in October 1987, when thirteen European countries signed a memorandum of understanding.

Nokia seized the opportunity to take an active part in the development of the technology of the GSM standard. It was very important that the standard Nokia focused on would gain a leading position globally. This was greatly helped when Radiolinja, the Finnish consortium of private telephone operators, had the distinction of opening Europe's first GSM network with equipment supplied by Nokia. In 1987 Nokia had formed a consortium with Alcatel and AEG to exploit mobile phones. Alcatel and AEG were at that time much bigger than Nokia, but they wanted the Finnish technology. This was another wise decision by Nokia; they got what they wanted—good access to European markets.

The people at the top had a lot to do with Nokia's phenomenal growth. Kairamo, in spite of his unfortunate end, had been an inspiring and charismatic figure who had emphasized the value of education, attracted a following of young lions, and had the vision of Nokia becoming a truly European company, a conglomerate. He foresaw the importance of securing inexpensive energy, the essential role of technical know-how based on research, and the value of political contacts, which he nurtured energetically. Ala-Pietilä, Alahuhta, Anssi Vanjoki (head of brand development), and Juhani Kuusi (head of the Nokia Research Centre) were key visionary figures after Kairamo's death. The competence they showed in their respective roles greatly facilitated the task of CEO Jorma Ollila in restructuring and reinventing the company after 1992.

Ollila's style was quite different from that of Kairamo. His background gave some clues as to how he would operate. From 1985 to 1990 he had been Nokia Group senior vice president, finance, then head of the Mobile Phones division in Salo from 1990 to 1992. His financial experience proved invaluable to Nokia when the company was listed on the New York Stock Exchange (NYSE) and was gaining access to international capital markets. Ollila's close familiarity with mobile phones also pointed him unerringly in the direction in which Nokia's fortunes were to prosper. When Ollila took over, Nokia was at an opportunity crossroads. Group operating profit at the end of 1991 was a minus figure, sales of mobile phones had barely taken off at less than one million units, and the continued diversification of Nokia industries clouded clarity of purpose. Where to concentrate?

The situation demanded a pragmatist of the first order, someone who would simplify and articulate key objectives, implement them single-mindedly, and follow through on all decisions. Ollila, a self-effacing but firm president, was such a man. He restructured and streamlined the organization, planned the firm's withdrawal from less profitable industries, and introduced a no-nonsense corporate culture that focused on productivity.

R&D became top priority for funding. Mobile phones, with a succession of value-adding new features, should become the company's core business focus. For all his overriding pragmatism, Ollila generated enthusiasm among his staff and made respect for the individual a key element in his mission statement. Finns like understated but committed realists who "do things right," however small. Ollila, shunning Kairamo's charismatic style, nevertheless showed acumen in his political contacts in Finland and in the world at large, and he has been eminently successful in welding together and maintaining his balanced leadership team.

The "Home Turf" Factor

Finnish institutional ownership of Nokia has shown a marked decline in the last decade. The growing brand awareness of Nokia, as well as the 1994 NYSE listing, has led to the company acquiring many characteristics of a U.S.-led group. In spite of the preponderance of foreign shareholders, however, Nokia has shown little inclination to move away from its Finnish home base. The completion of construction of the gleaming new company headquarters at Keilaniemi confirmed the management's desire to direct operations from the home turf.

In spite of Finland's somewhat remote geographical position, there are strong arguments indicating that the location is an advantage. Finnish technology, especially in electronics, is second to none, and the domestic market for Nokia's products was not only highly receptive, but played a part in spearheading development. Finnish industry has long excelled in the production of high-quality, well-designed niche products. Mobile phones were a perfect fit for the Finnish "small-but-good" concept and Nokia cleverly concentrated on lifestyle products that quickly acquired trend-setting features in Finland and the world at large. Significantly, Ericsson and Motorola failed to emulate this.

Education

In recent surveys Finland has been Number 1 in Europe in education levels, third in the world after Japan and Korea. This means that Nokia had a well-balanced workforce on its doorstep and was able to meet its recruitment needs locally for the critical R&D development.

When the Finnish Ministry of Education launched a supplementary education program for information technology in 1998, Nokia assumed a pivotal role, as well as donating substantial equipment to it. Although the company has had to attract a considerable number of recruits from foreign countries since the explosive growth of mobile phones, the supplementary IT education program ensures a fertile recruitment ground among Finnish graduates. Equality of opportunity in education for women has long been a reality in Finland, adding significant numbers to the potential local workforce; this fact should not be overlooked.

State Encouragement

The Finnish government has naturally lent support to the country's stellar enterprise. Tax treatment has not been punitive (Ericsson threatened to pull out of Sweden because of high taxes). Finland spends little money on military R&D, so more funds are available for industrial research. In 1981 the Finnish Licence Administration blocked Ericsson's exports to the Soviet Union from the Swedish company's Finnish subsidiary. The support of Radiolinja in placing the first GSM order was also a "home turf" factor.

The Finnish authorities can only be favorably impressed by the way Nokia has kept decision making and management in Finnish hands. A two-tier shareholding structure in the late 1990s resulted in 70 percent foreign stock ownership with only 16 percent voting power. Almost all Nokia board directors are Finnish, research and development is largely based in Finland, and most training takes place on Finnish soil.

Cultural Factors

The Finnish modus operandi—certainly successful in the case of Nokia—is, in essence, a culturally related phenomenon. Finns, living in a small state, have long been used to seeking out international markets and have developed language and other cross-cultural skills to facilitate this. Enterprising as they are, Finns functioning abroad refrain from pushiness or arrogance; their innate modesty and self-deprecatory manner gain them popularity across Eurasia, from Britain to Japan.

In the vast Asian markets (China, Japan, Korea, Malaysia, Indonesia) Finnish businesspeople are seen as reasonable, calm, non-aggressive, and trustworthy. In the United States, Finns enjoy the reputation of being honest and hard working and are considered good citizens. Nokia benefits from all this, where the client identifies the product with the likeable, trend-setting producer. In the IT era it's a good time to be Finnish. Perhaps it always was—Finns just didn't advertise it.

Advertising and design are other areas where Finns, and Nokia, have learned to excel. This too is related to Finnish cultural factors. While design in a series of Finnish products such as artistic glass, textiles, furniture, and modern architecture has long had a solid pedigree (Aalto, Saarinen, Sarpaneva, Franck, Wirkkala), the low-key, trendy Nokia ads, now seen worldwide, have been successful in cementing client approval. Like Nestlé and Coca-Cola before them, Nokia has used massive but tasteful advertising campaigns to create customer demand at the grassroots level.

Other inherently Finnish qualities—the freshness, open-mindedness, and adaptability typical of young people in a young country—have contributed significantly to Nokia's advancement. Flexibility and readiness to reinvent have been openly encouraged by Ollila and Ala-Pietilä—the speed at which the Mobile Phones division brings new models to market is bewildering. The life cycle of a mobile phone is just over two years and getting shorter.

Finns have proved they can adapt as needed to stay abreast with the modern era of changing, volatile demand for products. Their ability to be accurate and thorough is reflected in their steady progress toward production goals for handsets: production time has been cut from 40 minutes to 4 minutes; production start-up time, from 6 months to 1 month; number of mechanical parts reduced by 30 percent; testing time reduced by 50 percent. Finnish logistics skills were illustrated by an announcement in May 2000 by Kari-Pekka Wilska, president of Nokia Americas: "We must have

100 million components in the right place at the right time. And now we have."

It is a cultural characteristic of Finns that they operate confidently (and quickly) in a Finnish environment. This contrasts to some extent with Swedes, who tend to be somewhat nervous about fellow Swedes' opinions. Many of Nokia's managers went to the same schools and trust each other's judgment and back-up stance. Crises are confronted with typical Finnish calm and aversion to panic. Reliability is the highest-ranked quality in Finns' self-image.

A code of ethics permeates most of Finland's leading companies. Ranked as the world's least corrupt country, Finland is essentially law-abiding while at the same time being tolerant of occasional illicit behavior in other countries. The four basic values adopted by Nokia in the 1990s (customer satisfaction, respect for the individual, achievement, and continuous learning) reflected and exemplified Finnish values in the respect for the individual and the code of conduct vis-à-vis colleagues, customers, and society.

In summation, it is difficult to imagine a better setting for Nokia's sustained ascendancy than that of its home country. Finland is now an undisputed leader among nations in high technology. In this highly exciting and technically sophisticated environment, Nokia is well placed with its Global IP Mobility* concept to meet the daunting and kaleidoscopic challenges that will be posed by the future integration of two brave new ebullient worlds—multimedia wireless communications and the Internet.

In this important sphere of human activity and advancement, at least, it seems likely that Nokia Keilaniemi (and Finns) will continue to shape the world to come.

---

* A strategy under which Nokia would take a leading, brand-recognized role in creating the mobile information society

HOW TO APPROACH FINNS: A SUMMARY

With the object of making meaningful comparisons between different cultures, I have, in writing this book, made certain generalizations regarding the national characteristics of one people or another while spotlighting the Finns. Such generalizations carry with them the risk of stereotyping as one talks about the typical Italian, German, American, and so on. It is evident that Americans differ greatly from each other and that no two Italians are alike. However, my experience during thirty years of living abroad and rubbing shoulders with individuals of many nationalities has led me to the conviction that most of the inhabitants of any country possess certain core beliefs and assumptions of reality that manifest themselves in their behavior in specific ways according to cultural traits.

The English and the French have been close neighbors throughout modern history, but would anyone disagree that they differ as a group rather than just as individuals? Without committing oneself to absolute precepts, can it not be said that certain tendencies—French loquacity and pursuit of logic, British reserve and subtlety of humor, German thoroughness and sense of duty, American mobility and willingness to take risks—manifest themselves with admirable frequency in the hearts and souls of the people concerned?

These trends are, as I've said before, essentially relative: an articulate Dane will appear smoothly talkative to a Finn or a Norwegian, but the same Dane will be seen as a cold, reserved character by a Neapolitan or an Arab. The French consider themselves well mannered compared to Americans, but in Japanese eyes have rather earthy mannerisms at the dining table. All of us look to left or right, making judgments, drawing suspect conclusions—prisoners of our own historical traditions. National characteristics—generalized or not—are handed down through the centuries from one generation to the next and are perhaps most evident in those countries that have enjoyed an unbroken culture of long duration. The more consolidated a culture is, the less likely are its proponents to depart from its norms—which have destined them to survive and prosper. French historian François Guizot put it most clearly:

> When nations have existed for a long and glorious time, they cannot break with their past, whatever they do . . . they remain fundamentally in character and destiny such as their history has formed them. Even powerful revolutions cannot abolish national traditions . . . therefore it is most important, not only for the sake of intellectual curiosity, *but also for the good management of international relations,* to know and understand these traditions.

I was once in charge of an English language summer course in North Wales. We had assembled adult students from 3 countries—20 Italians, 12 Japanese, and 18 Finns. Intensive language instruction was relieved by social entertainment in the evenings and by the odd full-day excursion to places of scenic or historical interest.

We had scheduled a trip up Mount Snowdon on a particular Wednesday, but on Tuesday evening it rained heavily. Around ten o'clock that night, during the after-dinner dancing, a dozen or so Finns approached me and suggested that we cancel the excursion, as it would be no fun climbing the muddy slopes of Snowdon in heavy rain. I, of course, agreed and announced the cancellation. I was immediately surrounded by Italians, disputing the decision. Why cancel the trip? They had been looking forward to it (escape from lessons); they had paid for it in their all-inclusive fee. A little rain would not hurt anyone, and what was the matter with the Finns anyway? Weren't they supposed to be tough people?

A little embarrassed, I consulted the Japanese contingent. They were very, very nice. If the Italians wanted to go, they would go too. If, on the other hand, we cancelled the trip, they would be quite happy to stay in and take more lessons. The Italians jeered at the Finns, the Finns mumbled and growled, and eventually, in order not to lose face, agreed they would go. The excursion was declared on.

It rained torrentially all night and also while I took a quick breakfast in my room. The bus was scheduled to leave at half past eight; at twenty-five past, taking my umbrella, I ran to the vehicle in the downpour. Inside were sitting 18 scowling Finns, 12 smiling Japanese, and no Italians. We left on time and had a terrible day. The rain never let up, we lunched in clouds at the summit, and re-turned covered in mud at five o'clock in time to see the Italians taking tea and chocolate biscuits. They had sensibly stayed in bed. When the Finns asked them why, they said because it was raining.

I have related this experience because I believe it illustrates very clearly the strength of national mental conditioning. If some of the Italians had got on the bus, and if some of the Finns had stayed in bed, then one could have assumed that behavior depended on indi-vidual preferences. This was not the case: All the Finns felt they had to keep their word, no matter what. All the Italians exhibited the flexibility so typical of Latins. The Japanese also showed complete solidarity, in conformity with their collective instincts.

Your best starting point is to get it crystal clear in your mind that a Finn is a formidable person. The more one has to do with Finns, the more one realizes that they are, in effect, perfectionists. They defer politely to your cleverness or smoothness, but, in fact, they usually upstage you.

The upstaging is done discreetly, but effectively. Your modest Finnish partner, so complimentary of your own attributes, turns out to be a highly qualified technocrat with very solid assets. His office, car, and clothes may well be of better quality than yours; his house almost certainly will be. He has the highest standards in societal and professional living. Finnish managers insist on up-to-date technology, state-of-the-art factories and offices, training centers, sports facilities, and anything else that will increase productivity.

In Finland you can drink tap water; doctors know how to cure you if you are ill; buses, trains, and airplanes leave on time; there are no hurricanes. Newspapers are printed on high-quality paper, and the ink doesn't come off on your hands. Finnish milk and coffee are among the best in the world. Food is wholesome; society is solid. Finns possess a squat, flat-footed solidity that always makes you feel you know where you are with them.

Try to look solid in their eyes. Refer to your own culture's achievements, but always in a modest tone. A low profile works wonders with Finns; never boast. When you have said your piece, don't expect any feedback. They are thinking about what you have said. They don't think and talk at the same time. Enjoy the silence—not many people give you this luxury. Consider silence as a positive sign, and relax into it. Go to the sauna and have a drink.

Dr. Raimo Nurmi, in his cross-cultural note on Australian and Finnish values (1986), listed responsibility, capability, honesty, broad-mindedness, and independence as qualities Finnish university students said they admired most. This suggests that when working with Finns, you should try to set clear goals, define objectives, and appeal to the inner resources of the individual to achieve the task under his or her own steam—and to be fully accountable for it. Finns like to demonstrate their stamina in a lone task (note Finnish excellence in such lonely pursuits as long-distance running, skiing, and rally driving).

Finnish businesspeople wish to have both their responsibility and authority well defined. They don't want one without the other.

Self-discipline is taken for granted. Finns do not like being closely supervised; they prefer to come to you with the end result. You should listen well to Finns, for when they eventually have something to say, it is often worth listening to. You have to watch for subtle body language, as they have no other.

You may not oversell to them, but some charisma is okay. You can be humorous on any occasion, and you can talk about the cultural values of others, but don't praise the Swedes too much.

Finnish newspapers are among the best and most objective in the world, so Finns are probably better informed on most matters than you are. Show lively interest in Finnish culture—it is rewarding in any case. Make it clear that you know that Finland and Finnish products are high tech. If you are managing a Finn, remember his self-esteem is important and he does not necessarily solicit team support. He will sometimes be slow in making up his mind (he thinks deeply), but once it is made up, you are unlikely to succeed in changing it.

Bear in mind that Finns frequently exhibit originality. The uniqueness of their language and their outpost mentality encourage an independent outlook and lateral thinking, which enhance not only Finnish literature, music, and fine arts, but also extends to brilliance of industrial design and penetrative insight into various branches of technology. It is not by accident that Finland has, in recent times, figured among the foremost innovators in glass, textiles, furniture, imaginative shipbuilding, and electronic technology.

The Finnish manager, establishing a branch abroad, does not arrive with the heavy feet of the German or the sweeping, complacent logic of the French. Finns, especially men, may be regarded as a bit dull, or even gullible, but they are ready to learn and compromise.

Finnish businesswomen possess all the above qualities, but they are more talkative, open, and engaging. They are formidable allies or opponents, as they combine the thoroughness of the males with their own enthusiasm and exuberance. Foreigners can achieve a lot working in tandem with Finnish women, who thrive on recognition, respect, and imaginative projects. Reliability and accuracy are strong points—you can normally take these for granted.

Finally, remember that Finnish males (not so much the women) are very dry (this quality, too, brings its delights). The great Finnish composer, Jean Sibelius, who occasionally went on three- or four-day drinking sprees with other intellectuals, was once phoned by his long-suffering wife, who asked him for a forecast of when he might come back home. "My dear, I am a composer. I am involved in the business of composing music, not delivering forecasts," was the worthy man's reply.

FINLAND–PAST, PRESENT, AND FUTURE

The roller-coaster-ride nature of Finnish history raises interesting questions with regard to the country's future. Her international standing, internal settlements, and security arrangements are quite different from what they were prior to 1917. Has she done with the frowns of fortune? Is she now at the pinnacle of success? How will the Cultural Lone Wolf sustain the uniqueness of her national identity, now under threat not from Russian imperialism or communism, but from European economic integration or, worse still, insensitive globalization of products, consumer habits, rules and regulations, morals, trends, and policies? What will "Finnishness" mean in the middle of the twenty-first century?

The Past

Chapters 2 and 3 of this book have touched on the hardship, adverse conditions, and vicissitudes of life for premodern Finns. The transition from hunter-gathering in an inclement climate to a meager agricultural existence several centuries after it had taken hold in Southern and Central Europe was in itself a skimpy bonanza. From the twelfth century onward, Finnish peasants were subjects of two empires—subordinate, often feudal, but never subjugated and rarely humiliated. The chance political transformation of the Russian state opened the road to Finnish self-assertion and appeared to signal a turning point for the ill-starred nation. It proved to be so, but Finns were not yet out of the woods.

The sequence of events, predicaments, and international entanglements occurring between 1918 and 1945 stretched out in front of the young nation like an obstacle course at a track meet. The Civil War—bitter and acrimonious—was mercifully brief. The wars against the Soviets—crucial, menacing, last-ditch issues—were far more costly, especially in terms of human sacrifice and blood. The first two decades of independence witnessed severe economic depressions; the imposition of crippling war reparations was almost the last straw.

Through all these exigencies, the Finns showed they stuck to their principles, were resilient, and ultimately indomitable. By 1945 they had qualified as Europe's hero nation. The first twenty years of running their own affairs left them exhausted; they survived by the skin of their teeth. But it was in this period that they made their country. The years 1975–2000 would be pay-off time.

The Present

At the time of writing, the state of the nation is good. Complacency is not in fashion in Finland—perhaps never has been—but the country's achievements are substantial and visible. While the success of stellar enterprises such as Nokia, Kone, and Vaisala is well-founded and enduring, economic fortunes can wax and wane. However, other statistical indicators bode well for the country's future.

As things stand, Finland leads the world in environmental sustainability. This rating (compiled by *The Economist*) is based on indicators in five broad, durable areas: environmental systems, the reduction of environmental stress, the reduction of human vulnerability, social and institutional capacity, and global stewardship. Finland has a near-perfect record—only Norway, Canada, Sweden, and Switzerland come close. Within the framework of environmental sustainability, Finland is also the world leader in management of water resources—not surprising in view of her topography—a crucial asset in a world where the supply of water is rapidly becoming a survival issue. Another natural asset, the Finnish forest, is a lasting guarantee of national wealth. Finland is Europe's most heavily forested country (72 percent), and she maintains the viability of the forestry industry by judicious stewardship.

How competitive and durable is the Finnish economy? Again, indicators are impressive. Not only is Finland ranked in the top three for global competitiveness, but she is in first place in competitiveness based on the extent that a country is integrated into regional trade blocs. In this sense the Finnish business community shows a knack for nurturing policies that favor permanence. She leads Europe in economic creativity and research, being shaded worldwide only by the United States. Finland is unrivalled in various fields of technology and is number one in network readiness. Finally, taking into consideration her small population, the nation's gross domestic product (GDP) is stunning—thirty-first in the world, thirteenth in the world per capita, and fifth in the EU. Trailing in standard of living are the EU members United Kingdom, Ireland, the Netherlands, Belgium, France, Italy, Spain, and Greece, as well as a host of other prosperous countries such as Australia, Canada, Kuwait, Qatar, New Zealand, United Arab Emirates (UAE), Taiwan, South Korea, and Saudi Arabia. New entrants to the EU, such as Poland, Slovenia, Hungary, Slovakia, Czech Republic, and Estonia have GDPs per capita of less than half that of Finland and in most cases less than one-quarter.

Social and educational indicators are as solid as the economic ones. The welfare state has been a reality for many years. Medical practitioners and hospitals are of a high standard. Infant mortality is the third lowest in the world. Instances of crime, violence, terrorism, and drug abuse are low. Tertiary enrollment in universities and colleges is the highest in the world (a significant factor for future development), and a recent survey found Finns the most educated people in Europe. Another stabilizing societal factor is the preponderance of women in higher education and their full involvement in the political and commercial spheres.

The Future

If this brief audit of Finnish prosperity is comforting to friends of Finland, what are the chances of good fortune continuing in the next two or three decades? Current trends are not discouraging. Sad though it may be, rich countries tend to get richer and poor countries often poorer. Finland is by any standards a rich country today and may well see the gap widen between her standards and others' (even in a European context).

Another gap that tends to widen is the technological one. U.S. sophistication and advances in this area have been highly significant during the last twenty years. Again, Finland is well placed. The information era has proven favorable to the Finns, whose penchant for computers, electronic products, and love of gadgets has become legendary. Underpinning this foundation of technology is Finland's huge investment, at government and enterprise level, in research and development. This is bound to widen the technological gap between Finnish industry and those of many nations.

Investment of another kind—the funds and time spent on higher education—guarantees Finland a steady supply of well-trained graduates to fulfill the nation's requirements in industrial, commercial, and administrative fields. This also serves to keep the country's destiny (in the globalization age) in national hands.

Which leaves us with the question of the stability of Finland's position in the political arena as well as her ability to resist absorption into an identity-threatening, over-integrated "globalized" structure. Max Jacobson, Finland's former ambassador to the United Nations, has analyzed these issues in his penetrating, insightful book *Finland: Myth and Reality*. He discusses how national feeling, rather than being a declining influence or spent force, increased in importance during the last years of the twentieth century, when ideologies (particularly Marxism) began to crumble when faced with market realities. Wherever nationalism and ideology met head-on, nationalism triumphed.

The demise of communism in particular bolstered Finnish national confidence, born of the knowledge that in the Second World War only Britain, Russia, and Finland (in Europe) had not been occupied. Furthermore, Finland had been the only European nation to defend herself militarily with success. Jacobson, only too familiar with Finland's balancing act in the last century, points out that having been menaced by the East and let down by the West, she is now in a position to get the best from both sides. On the one hand, she is a respected member of the EU; on the other, she stands out as the only example of a Russian foreign policy success—a good neighbor; did Russia have another? Finland's role as key player between East and West can only serve to strengthen her security. After the dissolution of the Warsaw Pact bloc (to which Finland never belonged), she ended up in the bloc she wanted—the European Union.

Jacobson is only too well aware of the threat to national identities posed by international bodies such as the EU as well as the pressures emanating from huge commercial conglomerations. He sees Finns outliving these pressures, however, as their rugged independence would cause them to resist being governed from Brussels or swallowed up by the dictates of huge corporations. As I said earlier, Nokia, with only 6 percent of the shares held by Finns today, is run by a Finnish board of directors on Finnish soil. The company has a distinctive Finnish character, as do Kone, Finnair, and other Finnish enterprises.

My own opinion regarding the survival and continuance of a Finnish state "with a Finnish face" is based on my knowledge of the values and core beliefs of the people. Finnish values, as we saw in Chapter 6, are strong, quietly but passionately adhered to. Deep cultural values are hard to break or escape from. Individuals often do as they please, but nations rarely depart from their historic habits. In Finland, moreover, sweeping change is rendered difficult by the legislative structure. Finland has a unique brand of parliament, where new laws or changes can be enacted only by a two-thirds majority. There are no whimsical alterations in Finnish societal structure. Broad consensus must be obtained.

Finland (like Japan) is a member of many international organizations, but she retains traces of a Lone Wolf mentality. Secure inside the EU, she can maintain her equable relations with her giant neighbor to the East—no longer a viable threat. Indeed, an economically powerful Russia, perhaps entering the EU, would be the best possible development for Finland, as she would benefit enormously from trade, occupying a strategically central position in a (Greater) European Union.

In the twentieth century, Australia was known as the "Lucky Country." Certainly Finland was, as fate would have it, an unlucky one. Yet one can say that the Bolshevik Revolution brought her luck, and there may be some truth in this. Will Finland be one of the "lucky countries" of this century? Lucky or not, she has carved out her own destiny. She has fought her fight, paid her dues, and run her race—to the tape.

APPENDIXES

FINNISH HISTORY— CHRONOLOGY

9000 B.C.	Southern Finland becomes ice-free
8000 B.C.	Southern half of Finland colonized
7500 B.C.	Northern Finland reached
1000 B.C.	Baltic Finns arrive from area around Estonia
500 B.C.	Finns, Tavastians, Karelians, and Lapps vie for territorial advantage
1155	Swedes' First Crusade to S.W. Finland
1238	Swedes' Second Crusade to Häme
1293	Swedes' Third Crusade to the end of the Gulf of Finland
1323	Treaty of Pähkinäsaari between Sweden and Novgorod. Finland's eastern border set
1548	Michael Agricola translates New Testament into Finnish
1550	Helsinki founded
1642	Complete Bible published in Finnish
1721	Treaty of Uusikaupunki between Sweden and Russia
1776	First newspaper published in Finnish
1808	Russian invasion of Finland

1809	Sweden and Russia conclude Treaty of Hamina; Russia annexes Finland
1812	Capital moved to Helsinki
1835	*Kalevala* published
1860	Own currency established
1863	Language Manifesto; Diet begins to convene regularly
1878	Finland gets her own army
1899–1905	First period of Russification
1907	Finland obtains unicameral Parliament
1909–1917	Second period of Russification
1912	Finland wins nine gold medals at the Stockholm Olympic Games
1917	Finland declares independence December 6th
1918	Civil War 28th January—lasts three months Mannerheim assumes command of White Army. Victory in May
1919	Ståhlberg elected first president of Republic
1920	Peace treaty between Finland and Russia (Petsamo added to Finland)
1921	Compulsory military training enacted
1932	Finland and Russia sign nonaggression pact
1936	Finland finishes third in Berlin Olympic Games
1939	Russia attacks Finland 30th November; Winter War commences
1940	Winter War ends in March
1941–1944	Continuation War
1944	Finland drives out German forces from her territory Mannerheim becomes president for second time
1946	J. K. Paasikivi elected president
1952	Olympic Games in Helsinki; war reparations paid off
1956	U. Kekkonen elected president

1975	Helsinki Conference on Security and Cooperation in Europe
1982	M. Koivisto elected president
1989	Finland becomes member of Council of Europe
1994	M. Ahtisaari elected president
1995	Finland joins the EU
1999	Finland assumes presidency of EU
2002	T. Halonen elected president

Finland's Presidents

K. J. Ståhlberg	1919–1925
L. Kr Relander	1925–1931
P. E. Svinhufvud	1931–1937
Kyösti Kallio	1937–1940
Risto Ryti	1940–1944
C. G. E. Mannerheim	1944–1946
J. K. Paasikivi	1946–1956
Urho Kekkonen	1956–1982
Mauno Koivisto	1982–1994
Martti Ahtisaari	1994–2002
Tarja Halonen	2002–

INTERESTING FACTS ABOUT FINLAND

- Finnish radio broadcasts in Latin.
- The only foreign member of the Japanese Parliament is a Finn.
- Esa-Pekka Salonen is the chief conductor of the Los Angeles Philharmonic.
- Jukka-Pekka Saraste conducts the Toronto Symphony Orchestra.
- One of Finland's most popular bands is called the Leningrad Cowboys.
- The Finnish president lives in the former Palace of the Czar.
- Finland is known in the United Nations as the Super Peacekeeper.
- The Finnish people have public access to all the country's land.
- Finnish Lutherans attend church twice a year on average.
- Finns have a high median age—39.4 years.
- Finland has the third-smallest households in Europe (2.3 persons).
- Finns are proportionally the biggest users of libraries in the world—six million visits per annum.
- A Finnish couple won the World Tango Dancing Championship in 2000.

- Santa Claus lives at Korvatunturi, a mountain in Lapland. Concorde used to fly 40,000 visitors every December to see him.
- There are more saunas in Finland than cars.
- Finns spend more per capita on alcohol than any other people.
- Finns are the world's biggest coffee drinkers.
- Finland ranks among the top few countries for global competitiveness, economic creativity, environmental sustainability, network readiness, water resource management, minimal bureaucracy, and least corruption.

OLYMPIC MEDAL WINNERS—TOP 20
(Summer and Winter Games Combined)*

Country	Medal total	Per million inhabitants
1. Finland	531	106.0
2. Sweden	563	56.3
3. Norway	239	53.1
4. Hungary	442	44.2
5. Switzerland	275	38.7
6. Denmark	162	32.4
7. Australia	352	18.5
8. Austria	145	17.9
9. Netherlands	273	17.2
10. Cuba	145	15.2
11. Germany	1148	14.0
12. Britain	663	11.05
13. France	661	10.83
14. Canada	310	10.0
15. Italy	555	9.5
16. USA	2271	8.3
17. Poland	245	6.3
18. Soviet Union	1538	6.1
19. Japan	327	2.6
20. China	237	0.2

*Results up to but not including the 2004 Summer Games in Athens, Greece.

BIBLIOGRAPHY

Bookwell, W. S. 2000. *The Parliament of Finland.*

Cavalli-Sforza, L. L., et al. 1994. *The History and Geography of Human Genes.* Princeton, NJ: Princeton University Press.

Cavalli-Sforza, L. L., and A. Piazza. 1993. "Human genomic diversity in Europe: A summary of recent research and prospects for the future." *European Journal of Human Genetics* 1(3): 18.

Dolukhanov, P. 1989. "Prehistoric ethnicity in north-east Europe—comments on the paper by Milton G. Nuñez." *Fennoscandia Archaeologica.*

Guglielmino, C. R., et al. 1989. "Uralic genes in Europe." *American Journal of Physical Anthropology* 83:57–68.

Häikiö, M. 2000. "Nokia—The Inside Story." Helsinki: Edita.

Humphreys, Patrick. 2000. *Finland in a Small Book.* Helsinki: Yrityskirjat.

Jacobson, Max. 1987. *Finland: Myth and Reality.* Helsinki: Otava.

Julku, K. 1995. "Suomalais-ugrilaisten alkukodin ongelma." In *Rajamailla II,* edited by K. Julku, 134–53. Jyväskylä: Gummerus.

Klinge, Matti. 1987. *A Brief History of Finland,* 5th ed. Helsinki: Otava.

_____. 1977. *Sixty Years of Independent Finland.* Helsinki: Finnish-American Cultural Institute.

Nevanlinna, H. R. 1973. *Suomen Väestörakenne: Geneettinen ja Geneologinen Tutkimus.* Helsinki: Vammala.

Niskanen, M. E. W. 1998. "The genetic relationships of Northern and Central Europeans in light of craniometric measurements and gene frequencies." In *The Roots of Peoples and Languages of Northern Eurasia, I,* edited by K. Julku and K. Wiik, 134–50. Jyväskylä: Gummerus.

————. 1994a. "The origins and affinities of Finns and Saami (Lapps): Multidisciplinary approach." Paper presented at the American Anthropological Association Annual Meeting, Atlanta, Georgia.

————. 1994b. "An exploratory Craniometric Study of Northern and Central European Populations." Ph.D. dissertation. Washington State University.

Nuñez, M. 1987. "A model for the early settlement of Finland." *Fennoscandia Archaeologica* 4:3–18.

————. 1978. "On the date of the early Mesolithic settlement of Finland." *Suomen Museo* 1977:5–12.

Wiik, K. 1996. "Alkuperäiset ajatukseni." *Virittäjä.*

————. 1995. "Itämerensuomalaisten kansojen ja kielten syntykysymyksiä." Privately circulated manuscript.

ABOUT THE AUTHOR

Richard D. Lewis, who holds degrees in three modern languages from a British university and a Diploma in Cultures and Civilizations from the Sorbonne, has been active in the fields of applied and anthropological linguistics for over forty years. He first went to Finland for the Olympic Games in 1952 and has maintained a close relationship with the country since that time.

After the Helsinki Olympic Games, he worked for one year on a Finnish farm, learning Finnish and Swedish. On returning to the capital, he wrote articles for Finland's leading conservative newspaper, *Uusi Suomi*. In 1955 he founded the Berlitz School of Languages, Finland, in Helsinki, Tampere, Turku, Lahti, and Kotka. During this period he was tutor to Prime Minister Dr. Johannes Virolainen and other well-known Finnish figures such as Timo Sarpaneva and Viljo Revell.

In 1961 he pioneered the world's first English by Television series, produced by Suomen Televisio, which preceded the BBC's first series, *Walter and Connie* (1962), for which he was scriptwriter.

In the 1960s Richard Lewis traveled to all parts of Finland, wrote articles, lectured on Finnish subjects, and met Finns from all walks of life. In the 1970s, when Finnish industry began to internationalize, he organized language and cross-cultural courses for leading Finnish firms such as Nokia, Kone, Valmet, Neste, Orion, Ahlström, and Jaakko Pöyry. He also addressed cultural issues in seminars and lectures in Finnish, Swedish, British, U.S., and French universities and schools of business.

In the early 1990s he was asked to train the Finnish ministries in their preparations to enter the EU and subsequently carried out similar training for Swedish ministries.

His best-selling book *When Cultures Collide* (1996) is regarded as the classic work on cross-cultural issues. This was followed by *Mekö Erilaisia* (1997) and *The Cultural Imperative* (2003).

Richard Lewis is widely considered one of the world's most renowned interculturalists and linguists. He speaks ten European and two Asian languages and in 1999 was chosen as Personality of the Year by PATA (the Pacific Asia Travel Association) for his work carried out in relation to cultures in the Asia-Pacific area.

In 1997 Mr. Lewis was knighted by Martti Ahtisaari, the president of Finland, in recognition of his services in the cross-cultural field relating to the training of officials for EU entry (1995) and the EU presidency (1999).

INDEX

RICHARD LEWIS
COMMUNICATIONS

Richard Lewis Communications, Finland

Richard D. Lewis started operating in Finland in the 1950s, when there was a boom of interest in learning English for business. Traditionally, German and Swedish had been the main languages studied at school.

Since then, as Finns' English has improved immensely, there has been growing demand for communication skills and cross-cultural training. Over the years, many top business people and government officials have taken training with Richard Lewis Communications in Helsinki and around the country.

Thousands have also taken training courses with us in England at Riversdown House (near Winchester), London, and Billinge in the North West.

Whether you are a Finn, or one of the increasing number of people doing business with or living in Finland, we are here to help you get better results.

We teach all major world languages, including Finnish. We also teach and coach communication skills and offer a wide variety of cross-cultural training and support.

For further details, please contact us:

Email: info.finland@rlcglobal.com
Tel.: +358 9 4157 4700